African American Reparations

A roadmap for healing America and positioning the country for the future.

By Bryant W. Holt

DORRANCE
PUBLISHING CO
EST. 1920
PITTSBURGH, PENNSYLVANIA 15238

Dorrance Publishing Co
585 Alpha Drive
Pittsburgh, PA 15238
Visit our website at www.dorrancebookstore.com

ISBN: 979-8-88812-246-4
eISBN: 979-8-88812-746-9

DEDICATION

I dedicate this body of work to my grandson, Ra Beasley Holt. I love you, Abuelo.

TABLE OF CONTENTS

PREFACE

I am a descendent of American slaves. I believe it is overdue the nation has a real conversation about reparations for African Americans. There are two precedents of groups receiving reparations from the United States; the Japanese Americans for being incarcerated during World War II, and the Native Americans for their land seizure, massacre, and brutality. There is no secret that the founding fathers of the United States and planter-class owned African slaves. Many of these people were U.S. presidents and owned slaves' while they were in office. #1 George Washington (250 – 600), #2 Thomas Jefferson (200 – 600), #4 James Madison (100), #5 James Monroe (75), #7 Andrew Jackson (200), #8 Martin Van Buren and #9 William H. Harrison owned a single slave, but not while in office. #10 John Tyler (29), #11 James Polk (56), and #12 Zachary Taylor, the cousin of James Madison owned 300 slaves. Prior to the Emancipation, #17 Andrew Johnson owned nine slaves and Ulysses S. Grant owned a single slave, but not while in the office. There should be no debate that the effects of American slavery and the continuation of racism and discrimination negatively affected Black people hitherto. America must finally heal itself, and Black people must help lead the way. A new perspective is needed to facilitate African American self-determination and shape its brand of American patriotism. Despite centuries of discrimination against people of color in America, African Americans can help change their condition. However, to make the change will be a huge undertaking. While there have been many attempts in the past to bring about social justice for Black people, it has never been done with the acknowledgement and cooperation of the American people, as well as the unified support of Black people. My objective is to examine the challenges and pathway for African American reparations and seek input from the American people. I want to make it clear this is not an academic book, but more of a series of white papers used to illustrate an alternative perspective to go about reparations for Black people, I call it the **Manifesto of Emerging American Capitalism (MEAC)** which provides a roadmap. Is African American reparations possible? The MEAC will examine the complexities of African American unity and other issues of divisiveness that may serve as roadblocks. Also, the MEAC challenges the notion that Black people are monolithic and somehow limited to binary choices. I will not waste words launching into a diatribe against the United States, but instead, using straight talk to make an important point. It is my claim proposed in this roadmap reaffirms how business and market innovation could provide a way for African Americans to reconcile with America. During the coronavirus pandemic (COVID-19), I spent many hours examining my thoughts to formulate a prescription, I believe will improve the standing of Black people in the U.S. and on the world stage. I want to offer an alternative perspective to provoke discussions amongst the American people by revealing barriers that plague Black people from achieving the American dream. While the world stood still from COVID-19, people lived in isolation because normal life was placed on pause due to the disease and changed the way everyone thought about our society.

And for me, it became personal. Throughout my lifetime, African Americans were always isolated amongst themselves; a division that traces back to slavery. As much as people would like to stop talking about it, it is hard to break the chains of a slave's mindset, especially when it is constantly reinforced upon the consciousness of society. You can see it on television, at the movies and read on social media portraying Black people as victims and downtrodden. It is time for leaders to emerge, leaders who can rally Black people towards a common vision and purpose. I believe it is possible for African Americans to become a transformational force for good and create an economic engine that uplifts its communities by changing how Black people are perceived to the world. For that to happen, America must look beyond the distractions of political pundits and seek ways for the country to heal and become stronger than ever! There has always been division and turmoil in the United States; from the American Revolution, African Slavery, to World Wars. And recently, so much has happened in the country, especially, given the coronavirus pandemic that fostered in an era of widespread misinformation. It is not clear to many people who to believe in anymore. Between right- and left-wing political talking points and propaganda has divided the country amongst large swatches of America, especially amongst its working poor. Despite the vast differences amongst the American people, I still believe America is the greatest melting pot society in the world and represents a beckon of light shining on a hill for all people to prosper. But, if we continue to degenerate into a house divided, America will surely fall. Many people across the socio-economic spectrum are experiencing the wealth gap, and African Americans has the highest inequities compared to other groups.

Most people agree the government's attempt to rectify these circumstances has failed and continues to offer false hope. The passage of the **U.S. Bipartisan Infrastructure Law (BIL)** was a great idea for the country but flawed and destined to fall short of its intent. The government is too large to effectively target money to those who really need it. Idealistic programs, supposedly aimed at eradicating poverty and social inequality, often promoted by liberal progressive leaning politicians are short-lived. In most cases, their national narratives are made up of empty promises to pacify a few token leaders. It will surely keep reparations off the national conversations. Conversely, racism still exist, and their racist sympathizers are hell bent on disrupting racial harmony in the country. Black people should not be distracted about debating whether to dismantle Confederate monuments, but instead address the elephant in the room and decide how to resolve African American unification. Rather than tearing down or removing Confederate statues, let's erect new statutes of prominent African Americans adjacent to or across from them to show the evolving history of the country. Removing and defacing monuments or eliminating slavery from school curriculums are all forms of book burning in my opinion. No one wins and everybody loses. While it is unlikely the U.S. will breakout into another Civil War along racial lines in my lifetime, there is a need to combat the resurgence of White Supremacy throughout western countries. As a society, we need to bridge the gap between the poor (White and Black) people and the wealthiest in the country, or risk further deterioration of the American middle-class, like the French Revolution did to France in 1787.

People are asking, how did we get here? It is clear the erosion of middle-class jobs served as the precursor to creating the wealth gap between the rich and poor, especially amongst the Black minority and the White working poor. For change to happen, our political leaders and their pundits must stop dividing the country. If you look at the behavior of our two-party political system and their media machines, it is hard to foresee reparations. There are rising tensions between the U.S. and other superpowers, as geopolitical foes like China and Russia have become embolden by openly taking aim at the U.S., claiming America is racist and that the zenith of its influence is over. We should remember Rome was not conquered – it imploded from within. It is true, China is modernizing its infrastructure at a high rate, while America's infrastructure is aging and deteriorating, partially due to a growing unrest and political infighting. I still believe the U.S. democracy is the best in the world. Contrary to China' assertions, I would argue that the American experiment is a work in progress, as the U.S. still control much of trade in the world, albeit with bourgeoning debt and a weakening democracy. Americans' intellectualism and wisdom cannot succumb to fear, as fear will debilitate its ability to include all its people to advance critical thinking. During the BIL negotiations for the $1.2 trillion appropriations, it was unfortunate that not a single person of color participated in the discussion.

After the passage of the BIL in the U.S. Congress, it is not clear the American people understood how the funds will be spent. The MEAC sets out to make the case for how the BIL could facilitate African American reparations. While it will not require any new spending, it will require an acknowledgement on the part of Congress to appropriate future provisions for African American reparations, marking a new era for the United States of America. African Americans were used to help build the early infrastructure of the United States for free, and now America has an opportunity to facilitate compensation in rebuilding the needed new infrastructure. African Americans have lost generations, and in some cases, brilliant people who might have made a difference in the world. The MEAC lays claims that the realization of climate change is real, and mitigation and resiliency initiatives are needed in urban areas. The emergence of space travel and exploration will require a new breed of entrepreneurs, thinkers, scientists, and pioneers. If America is willing to allow all its citizens to participate in our great experiment, then the BIL may serve as the catalyst to ignite a social movement to unite America and bring healing to the country. It could enable African American reparations and reinforce American exceptionalism. Nothing I write about is original. I do not claim to be unique. I happen to live during a time where historical and current events can be seen more clearly. I have arranged known and accepted facts in a practical way for common-sense understanding. Also, I must admit I am not a religious person, but I have always considered myself spiritually minded. Christians claim to believe in the sovereignty of God; and cannot serve God and Mammon at the same time. I heard some Christians say it is God's plan to determine if reparations for Black people will ever materialize. I think, before God can do his work, there must be a plan set in motion to follow. I cannot imagine how something so insurmountable like African American reparations to occur without the support of its people.

I don't know exactly how it will happen or when it will happen, but it is my hope that the American people will weigh in and bring their voices to the conversation. I anticipate all sorts of reactions, from exuberance and engagement from certain quarters of the country to ambiguity and disinterest with other quarters, to absolute antagonistic and counter-strategist to round out the balance. For me seeing the results in my lifetime is of little concern since my part only involved establishing the framework for America's consumption. It is up to the American people to decide. I prepared four white papers to illustrate how America might go about African American reparations and facilitate socio-economic equilibrium. These papers are intended to be evergreen, where future contributors are encouraged to build on the text and advance the principles and purpose of African American reparations. I want to be clear it is not because of a lack of intelligence that Black people find themselves in their predicament, but an inability to build on an enduring foundation and framework for which a common platform of unification can be achieved. I believe Black people are entering a period of enlightenment and ready to overcome the circumstances that eluded them for centuries. I thought about how Black Americans could mirror successful immigrants to help shift their mindset. Unfortunately, thinking of African Americans as immigrants is a false premise. First, the basis of any enduring and stable group of immigrants, is their community and institution were built on a strong unified group. There is strength in numbers. And their people are aligned to build a solid base that accounts for its entire population. Otherwise, there is no survival of future generations if they fail to plan and organize at the granular level.

The foundation is at the heart of African American reparations. Without the consensus of the American people, and Black people in particular, reconciliation of our nation will remain essentially out of the realm of the American consciousness. Secondly, successful immigrants established a strong foundation aligned around accountable and responsible people who accomplished great things. These immigrant communities living in America understood what it takes to sustain their communities; valued and supported by other communities, and own by people who live in their communities. Many immigrants came to the U.S. to startup businesses with many barriers to market. Despite coming to the country with advanced education, they were discriminated against and forced into lesser niche markets. Eventually, their descendants were able to branch out into to other disciplines and emerge into other enterprises becoming real power brokers in the region. If African Americans come to account for their own destiny as a people and determine the outcome of their own success, the American people will come to truly accept and recognize them for their persistence, endurance, and humility. Thirdly, the earnings from the enterprises developed by these immigrants were reinvested back into their community in such a way that these communities redefined the very landscape, from language and cultural traditions to the names of streets, and buildings in the neighborhoods. Over time and without fanfare, an entire city takes on a completely different complexion empowered with all the political influence and power that comes with it.

Organized immigrants demand inclusion and ensure their people are heard by the people in power. America respects a winner, especially winners of a great comeback story. There have been many stops and starts for Black people over the course of American history. For Black people, it appeared all is loss, and at the precipice of despair and isolation. African Americans must quietly redefine its role in America. Fourthly, to sustain the building blocks of the community, other social services and social networks are formed to ensure the gains are maintained, relearned, and handed down to the youth in the most formal and public manner possible. Their people's historical narrative is highly encouraged. Their ability to build something from nothing provided confidence for them to lead their people and others, thus, preparing them to control their own territory right here in America! I am interested to hear what the American people think successful reparations looks like. The MEAC must transcend the dross of materialism and human ego. While I acknowledged there have been many individual accomplishments of wealth, fame, and prestige amongst Black people, I humbly must debunk the notion that African Americans were ever afforded equal opportunities to pursue the American dream. There will come a time when the veil of deception is lifted so all can see where we've come from as a nation. As the author, I believe my purpose is to propose this alternative for others to scrutinize and decide if they want to make it real. Clearly, African Americans are not, nor have ever been considered immigrants. They were enslaved people, systematically dehumanized for centuries.

The disingenuous attempts of the government programs to rectify the wrongs done to Black people falsely adopted a belief that reparations were somehow achieved. Despite the injustice against Black people, African Americans accomplished great things throughout American history, and at the highest level of society. However, it is not enough for a few individuals to stand alone, become wealthy, and yet be a part of a powerless group. America and African Americans must keep in mind that great civilizations were built on pluralism, and not individualism per se. Black people are said to have been asleep for over four hundred years but are now awake and aware of their true condition. It is time for the sleeping giant to wake up and take your place at the table. It is no longer the responsibility of outsiders to make reparations a reality. Many have tried and failed so there are no illusions that this approach will be any different, but there is no harm in laying out the argument and conclusion once and for all if such a monumental movement could happen. I challenge America to demonstrate to the world how exceptional we are as a people and as a nation by forging the greatest comeback story in its history – the restoration of dignity for the descendants of the American slaves and correcting America's past. For Black people, it will mean no more barriers (real or perceived) to prevent full participation in the American experiment. Because the United States never healed from Slavery or the Civil War, we need a movement capable of fostering and inspiring a new vision by which all Americans can rally behind to bring resolution once and for all! It would be a travesty to omit any parts of American history or promoting sedition against the United States of America, as this will severely damage our national franchise.

I am not convinced we explored all the options for reconciliation with the people of America. The movement of African American reparations must begin with small groups of people weighing in on the conversation. As with the founding fathers, whose primary mission was to empower a nation and leave an impenetrable and sustainable institution, so is true in this case.

The book offers an alternate perspective about American capitalism and how Black people can use it to achieve reparations. The book discusses an African American reparations roadmap described in the following white papers: 1) Form of a Foundation that focuses on overcoming major challenges facing African American's fragmented community, confronting the African American unity dilemma, as well as espousing for an African American narrative of patriotism. 2) Create an Enterprise that focuses on the corporate ownership and African American institutions. 3) Reimage Markets that African Americans can drive value innovation through market disruption to improve existing or develop new products and services, while maintaining high levels of quality and ways to enhance the customer experience. 4) Build a Basecamp that lays out the groundwork for the Black community human infrastructure plan. And finally, 5) Have the national Conversation with the American people, via a call-to-action. The world is watching to see what comes next as the American people faces our darkest sins and accept our role in the present tense to seek salvation by solving reparations for African Americans together.

Clearly, the country is still struggling with the matter. Now that we have matured as a nation, it is time to address the issue in a very public way. That means looking at reparations through a variety of lenses. For example, it will not be easy for Black people to overcome generations of subjugation and victimization to thinking big and believing anything is possible. For White people, it will be equally difficult to divorce themselves from a privileged mindset and superiority to being open-minded, sharing how you think the American people might consider reparations. Unpacking the MEAC in a safe environment will provide the American people with an opportunity to strengthen the argument for African American reparations and finally bringing closure to the American Slave era. I asked for the readers to organize into book clubs and send your feedback as part of my "Call to Action" discussed in the closing chapter of the book. I believe the book club discussions will serve as an ongoing forum to engage people across America to offer their point of view, and remain confidential. This national conversation will give all Americans an opportunity to say something about it. To have an effective conversation, you must be willing to approach the topic with an open mind. Send your responses to the author or share your comments on social media. It is my hope that the national conversation will engage the American people to develop a framework for the African American Reparations Act of 2030 we can all support.

"When we are debating an issue, loyalty means giving me your honest opinion, whether you think I'll like it or not. Disagreement, at this stage, stimulates me. But once a decision has been made, the debate ends. From that point on, loyalty means executing the decision as if it were your own."

Gen. Colin Powell

THE FOUNDATION

During 1909, W.E.B. DuBois, Mary White Ovington, Moorefield Storey, and Ida B. Wells were the social movement leaders of their time, recognizing the importance of collective thought and cooperation amongst African Americans. They assembled great legal minds and intellectuals to form the National Association for the Advancement of Colored People (NAACP) assembled to address civil rights and injustices against Black people.

In my opinion, the legacy of African Americans is to leave their children better off than before. The end game in life is goodwill towards mankind. The Declaration of Independence stated it best that we the people have an inalienable right to life, liberty, and a pursuit of happiness. While the founding fathers that authored the document were flawed, their words were pure.

All societies, and more importantly, their leaders, are fallible since people are motivated by self-centeredness and tempted by flesh. Each generation must learn to build upon a strong foundation and continue to do good work. By achieving self-reliance and cooperation amongst most of the American people is paramount. It will take a vision and real leadership to earn the respect from other cultures and from other Black people to support an equitable African American reparations agenda.

The conflict between good and evil is a constant challenge amongst the American people since the abolition of slavery. The stereotypes inflicted upon Black people have been debilitating to the psychology of the individual and proven destructive to the entire race. Some people use the term, "woke" to describe someone who advocate an extreme view of the social injustices and structural racism wedged against a less significant group of people. African Americans must move passed being awakened to being enlighten about what to do. Regardless of one's racial and ethnic background, the goal is to win the hearts and minds of the American people to support a common purpose.

THE FOUNDATION

- PREFACE
- INTRODUCTION
- CHRONICLE OF AFRICAN AMERICANS
- THE AFRICAN AMERICAN UNIFICATION DILEMMA

PREFACE

It will never be a good time for the American people to discuss African American reparations legislation. Not just older Americans, but young people too. Regardless of their race and ethnicity, people are cynical about the government and lack confidence in the political process because they do not believe voting makes a difference. This may explain the divisiveness between the two- party system. Even seasoned Black voters share similar sentiments since they have seemingly been down this road before, only to see the same slow pace of change. To say that the 2020 Presidential Election was one of the most crucial elections of our lifetime is a political talking point because every political cycle represents a continuous referendum of the United States' promise to make this country a more perfect union. If Black people get distracted by manufactured sideshows, they will lose sight of the ultimate prize. To not vote in any election is unacceptable, especially when you think about those early freedom fighters, women, Black and White people who lost their lives to give all people the right to vote. It is not the time for false arguments of indifference. There are people in control who want nothing more than for the masses to lose their will, to quit, as voter suppression, fake news and other schemes are used to complicate matters and make the process overwhelmingly difficult.

Throughout my life, I learned how to apply my innate gifts to reify and build consensus; an ability to create order out of chaos and shape abstract ideas into something tangible and understandable. I believe the ultimate form of African American reparations is readiness. Black people will achieve success only when they are prepared to receive it. First comes planning, followed by organizing, and then executing. I believe African Americans need a wholistic governing body of the people. A foundation is needed to assemble the building blocks towards institutional wealth and political influence. Don't be fooled into thinking that the MEAC is about getting rich at all costs.

The ghetto economy of selling illegal substances, gambling and prostitution is not sustainable. Even legal ways like singing and dancing; hitting, kicking, bouncing, and throwing a ball may get you fame and fortune, but the careers will eventually end. The wealth of these people will disappear after they are gone, providing little benefits to their community. There is no succession plan for institutional wealth to sustain and promote Black people in the United States, and this is why Black people continue to lag other groups. If African Americans depend on the U.S. government alone to secure reparations, it will prolong the likelihood of successful implementation, as government support always come with strings attached. Historically, the early laws in the United States were written by and for White men solely for the purpose of protecting their assets and to maintain control over their property. The founding fathers created structural barriers to prevent others from participating in the process despite the Declarations of Independence and the U.S. Constitution.

The notion of having Black people on the inside of government institutions would eventually change policy to make a difference is a good thought but fall short of its intent. Without power or influence they are compelled to follow the same established rule of law and ordinances they were trained to administer, making them complicit. Until Black people can demand changes to the laws to benefit their constituents, nothing will change. A foundation would embody a group of principled people who would come together for the purpose of implementing a roadmap how African Americans can chart a new course guided by institutions and operatives to serve and sustain their interest in the long run. Despite the devastating setbacks leveled against Black people throughout American history, the embers from the dampen flame persist. Black people have gone through the five stages of grief and must now persevere until their resolve to unite its people is assured. I believe the long-standing endurance of Black people could produce an outcome worthy of epic proportion.

A foundation can help change the trajectory of future generations in a way that manifest a new African American consciousness. The African diaspora is a little different from other people who were separated from their homeland to re-settle into new lands. For Black people in America, the diversity of enslaved African tribes and racial intermixing complicates matters significantly. All earlier attempts of African Americans to create roots in America have been met with rejection and confrontation. The foundation concept is less about overcoming racial disparities and petitioning for equality, and more about empowering people to take control, coupled with a strategy to help people take matters into their own hands and fulfill the promise of land and establishing the tangible Black community. To be clear, the foundation is about strategizing a way to build the framework for Black structural institutions. It is not about seeking revenge or revolting against the United States. The goal is to move African Americans collectively closer to the promises of the country to achieve their full potential and contribute to our society. The foundation starts the national conversation by exploring the chronicle of African Americans and the challenges to unite its people. A strict adherence to my suggestions is not required, but highly recommended. Afterall, Black people have been down this road before and continuing to do the same thing repeatedly and expect a different result is by all account the definition of insanity. African Americans must stop the madness of debating one another and confront the true nature of its limitations. The future of Black people may rest in the next generations' survival, but the legacy of the current generation must lay the foundation to ensure its destiny.

Achieving unity amongst Black people will be the single most challenging hurdle to overcome because African Americans are so fragmented, especially when it comes to their riches and support of one another. They have not realized the immense power of the collective, and using their wealth, politics, and social narrative as levers to fine tune the co-existence of its people.

INTRODUCTION

First, let's begin by examining the first hurdle of African American reparations, and that starts with Black people themselves. The MEAC offers a new perspective to enable the transformation and reconciliation of Black people from their current condition. African Americans must come to cultivate their own institutions. Because market conditions fluctuate, especially in urban areas, the need to amass a portfolio of businesses to counteract these limitations is crucial. The foundation can learn from other successful economic structures used in other emerging markets that formed conglomerates to benefit its society. The foundation's stewards must adhere to high standards of integrity. The foundation must be sophisticated enough to distinguish between ideology and religiosity, so as to embrace the secular population and avoid conflating the mission, market goals, and objectives. The ultimate by-product is to create wealth, prosperity with autonomy to change the course of future generations of Black people. Imagine stable national African American institutions based in the United States where Black people work, play, and live built on their ingenuity. The MEAC proposes an African American financial strategy based, in part, on the Japanese Keiretsu economic structure. The brain-trust must manage an organizational structure based on professional conduct and legal binding agreements to ensure legitimacy amongst economies around the world, and its investors. These Black institutions must have universal appeal that systematically benefit African American communities. According to Maslow's theory of human psychology, people have five primary needs that include security, food, and shelter. After achieving basic needs, people seek out relationships of love and belongings. If their emotional connections are satisfied, they look outwardly to find validation of one's self-esteem. Upon achieving recognition for their accomplishments, they shift to the highest state of human psychology, according to Maslow, is to achieve self-actualization, as they look beyond themselves to do for others. Throughout the spectrum of human existence, society must strive to facilitate these important requirements. Every American wants the same thing out of life, and that's the ability to provide for their family in pursuit of harmony and peace.

While these may seem basic rights for most Americans, these virtues have long eluded disenfranchised African Americans. The time has come to bring our country closer together as Black people lift their community. The decision-makers who impact major urban centers and surrounding suburbs are misguided when it comes to African American's self-determination. American security systems, food sources, and real estate development were originally directed towards the city's core, and then into sprawling rural townships, leaving a trail of abandoned buildings and shrinking White populations. Today, with the advent of eCommerce, affluent suburbs are losing older White populations to areas farther out, and younger White people are retreating to gentrify downtown center cities, adding to a surplus of abandoned buildings and underutilized properties. Black people cannot continue to follow from behind, or risk being left in "no mans" land.

U.S. taxpayers continue to spend billions of dollars on building new infrastructure in the outer regions instead of refurbishing the highly efficient infrastructure already established in central metropolitan areas. Entrepreneurs across the United States recognized the phenomenon of the "Build and Abandon" syndrome and are figuring out how to bring urban and adjacent suburban cities back to life. African American entrepreneurs can seize this opportunity by building from the suburbs back into the cities.

The MEAC is aimed at cultivating relationships amongst all Americans, but especially for Black people to unite and drive action. The melting away of African American blackness is not an excuse for indecision, nor will running away into the abyss of multiculturalism will solve African American reparations. It is time for responsible, principled, knowledgeable, and influentially competent Black people to clear the way and demand change. That mean changing everything as we know it, to redefining, orchestrating, and sustaining an entirely new narrative for African Americans. Before amassing economic power, influencing public perception, and charting a new direction with a more predictable outcome, will require everyone to get on the same page. And here lies the challenge.

It is difficult for any people to unite following the trauma of wars and slavery. The collateral damage is defeat and unbridled subjugation with no other option but to assume the beliefs and characteristics of their captors.

Dating back to the ancient times, African empires were the target for territorial wars resulting in the loss of their land with the invasion of the Ottoman empire into northern Africa. They eventually overpowered and subjugated northern Africans into slavery and taught them Arabic and Persian language and indoctrinated them with Islamic religion. In the sub-Sahara Africa, many African countries fought amongst each other, either at the behest of their colonizers, or because of tribal fighting over territory and trade.

Eventually, the Portuguese and other Europeans would take part in dismantling these Africa countries. The entire continent was craved up by western colonial powers to seize control over vast natural resources and minerals, as well as subjugating African people and forcing them to adopt their language and religion.

During the colonial slave trade era, Africans from various tribes were captured and sold into slavery bound for the United States and elsewhere. These Africans spoke many different languages and had different traditions. To further destabilize their tribal connections, family members were split and sold separately. The syndrome of captivity spawn distrust, uncertainty, and despair, imposed by the slaveowners, explains in part, the unity issue amongst Black people who descended from the enslaved people.

CHRONICLE OF AFRICAN AMERICANS

Allow me to establish a common understanding of the American enslaved people and their journey to post-slavery America. Because of African American scholar, Lerone Bennett, Jr., we learned a lot about how the United States began the journey into one of the darkest periods of its history. The European Conquest and **Colonial Slave Trade** enslaved nearly 9.2 million African people and exported them throughout the Americas to a life of servitude and brutality. The United States origin took shape during the **American Revolution** (1775-1783), where early American rebel soldiers fought against Great Britain. According to historical records, Africans fought on both sides, but about 9,000 Africans or four percent fought as Patriots, and 5,000 were combat troops amongst the total 250,000 soldiers and militia who served the American cause during the revolutionary war. The colonies eventually declared their independence from Great Britain on July 4, 1776. The official signing occurred in 1783 at the Treaty of Paris with Britain. From the very beginning, freed African Americans played an important role in shaping the new world, as notable, Benjamin Banneker, helped survey the plans of the new capital city of the United States in the District of Columbia, Washington, DC in 1791. The **War of 1812** ensued when Britain began to block American trade to prevent U.S. expansion into British territory. After the U.S. forced Britain to give up its territory on the North American continent, it precipitated a conflict with the Seminole Native American tribe along with Black people from the Spanish Florida Everglades under the **Indian Removal Act 1830** (aka, Trails of Tears). Later the U.S. entered the **Mexican War** (1846-1848) annexing Mexico territories, which is now Texas, Nevada, Arizona, New Mexico, and Utah. Mexico lost two-fifths of its country because of U.S. military dominance. By 1800, approximately 893,600 Africans were condemned to slavery. By 1860, according to U.S. census, there were over 3 million African people sold into slavery in southern United States. Life for enslaved African people during the **Antebellum Period** were subjected to miscegenation and confined to perform back-breaking labor on large plantations, small farms, and as house servants. Slavery, in the United States was considered a legal institution and widely enforced throughout the south during the Colonial Era leading up to the civil war. During the **Abolitionist Movement**, freedom fighters like Nat Turner who led the uprisings before the Civil War and Frederick Douglas who worked alongside White abolitionists which led to the U.S. Supreme court Dread Scott decision in 1857 before the Civil War to free Africans from slavery. History would not be complete without mentioning the role of Harriet Tubman in the Underground Railroad to help Africans escape from southern plantations. Slavery was the root cause of the **American Civil War,** (1861 – 1865). President Abraham Lincoln (#16), had to dismantle slavery because it was a threat to the economic interest of the industrialize north versus the slave's free labor market of the south. The southern planter class was emboldened because they grew accustomed to the cultural values of White supremacy and privilege and opposed the growing power of the federal government to control the states. The end of the Civil War marked the surrender of the southern Confederacy government in practice only. To help secure their freedom, African slaves were used to fight against the confederacy in exchange for the so-called 40-acres and mule agreement.

The Union Army issued field order #15, on January 16, 1865, contrived by General, William Tecumseh Sherman, and Secretary of War, Edwin M, Stanton. The agreement was constructed into three sections; the first provision set apart a settlement for freed Africans, the second provision proclaimed that the African settlement would be self-governed, and third provision stated that each family shall have a plot of 40 acres of tillable land. The **Emancipation Proclamation** was to grant freedom to the slaves in the Confederate states if the states did not return to the Union by January 1, 1863. In addition, under the proclamation, freedom would only come to the slaves if the Union won the war.

The Proclamation itself freed very few slaves. Eventually, the Emancipation Proclamation led to the proposal and ratification of the **Thirteenth Amendment to the Constitution** (January 31, 1865), which formerly abolished slavery throughout the land. But it wasn't until June 19, 1865, known as **Juneteenth,** when 2000 Union Soldiers entered the confederacy territory of Galvin Bay, Texas to make the announcement to 250,000 enslaved people that they were free people by executive decree. The United States Congress recruited freed slaves under the Army Organization Act in 1866, where they formed six all Black cavalry and infantry regiments to control Native Americans of the Plains, capture cattle rustlers, and protect settlers, stagecoaches, as well as railroad crews along the western front. The Native Americans gave them the moniker, Buffalo Soldiers. Right after the Civil War, well before the Great Migration, more than 26,000 freed Africans left the southern states and settled in the Great Plains to establish agricultural communities known as Nicodemus Farmers. The United States continued to struggle following the Civil War, as the country sought to reintegrate those southern states that seceded from the Union and failed to recognize the legal status of African Americans during the **Reconstruction Era** (1863 - 1877). The Reconstruction failed because of weak legislation and did nothing to protect former slaves from persecution, and ultimately did not bring about fundamental change to the social fabric of the South. Even after being handicapped by enslavement, many African Americans descendants of former slaves emerged and contributed to the advancement of American ingenuity. Take for example, Inventor, Elijah McCoy, whose parents were former slaves from Kentucky, escaped to Canada during the Underground Railroad Movement. McCoy traveled to Scotland to study Mechanical Engineering. He is most notable for developing an automatic lubricator that spreads oil evenly over locomotive and ship engines while still moving. His invention led to the design for new engine lubrication systems of the early 20th century. Another Black inventor, Andrew Beard, made improvements to locomotives by designing the automatic railroad car coupler. The basis of his design is still being used today. Despite the achievements of individual African Americans, inclusion would remain in the balance because Black people had no political power, as they could not vote, and did not have a way of communicating to the masses of their people in a concerted way. In 1847, some Blacks resettled in West Africa due the political and racial tension in the United States. Liberia was established by the U.S. Government, and the capital city was called Monrovia, named after U.S. President James Monroe (#5). The country was destined for failure since it was ruled by the same colonizer from America.

For those Blacks who decided to remain in the U.S. would go on with the struggle to influence people throughout the world, making strong arguments for freedom and human rights, something that would elude them for another hundred years.

The failure of the Reconstruction period led to the **Jim Crow Era** (1877-1954), where a collection of states enacted laws to legalized segregation policies supported by an institution of racism administered by the Ku Klux Klan (KKK). For nearly 100 years after the Civil War and the elected offices of fifteen U.S. Presidents, from Rutherford B. Hayes (#19) to Woodrow Wilson (#28) and Harry Truman (#33), African Americans were continuously marginalized and subjugated, being denied the right to vote, access to education, and prevented from holding good jobs. Those who defied Jim Crow laws faced arrest, fines, jail sentence and lynchings. One could safely say this is structural racism. Can you imagine what African Americans had endured during this period? Now imagine at the height of Jim Crow, in 1902, where a group of wealthy Black people (e.g., O.W. Gurley - landowner, J.B. Stradford – lawyer/hotel owner, and A.J. Smitherman – founder of the *Star* newspaper) defied all logic and purchased land and built businesses in a segregated section of Tulsa, Oklahoma. They would eventually establish an economic power base along Greenwood Avenue lined with office buildings, luxury shops, restaurants, hotels, salons, and nightclubs that became known as Black Wall Street. This affluent African American community is a story most Americans never hear or read about in its history books; where between May 31st and June 1, 1921, an angry mob of people massacred hundreds of Black people and burned down their businesses leaving an untold number of people homeless. They were amongst the settlements that traveled to Oklahoma to control their own economy, politics, and narrative nearly a hundred years ago, but the country wasn't ready. Throughout the Jim Crow era, African Americans faced untold barriers making their life a living hell in America. Moreover, the U.S. Supreme Court ruled in 1896, Plessy versus Ferguson, that racially segregated public facilities were legal. After the declaration of **World War (WWI),** which took place between 1914-1921, more than 20,000 Black people enlisted. When the Selective Service Act was passed in May 1917 and documented on July 5, 1917, over 700,000 African Americans had registered for military service. The war efforts were complicated by the deadly Influenza virus, known as the Spanish Flu pandemic of 1918. One-third of the world's population (500 million globally), and 675,000 people in the United States died from bacteria pneumonia. While Black people suffered lower morbidity rates than Whites between September – November of 1918, Black people had higher fatalities than the White population. After WWI, 6,000,000 African Americans moved from rural Southern United States to the urban Northeast, Midwest and West during the **Great Migration**, or Great Northward Migration of 1916, and continued up to 1970. Because of the poor economic conditions in the Jim Crow south, Black people believed they could provide a better life for their families by working in the factories spurred by the manufacturing expansion in the north. Unfortunately, they were not welcomed with open arms, as unknowing to African Americans would face housing discrimination, low employment opportunities and separate public accommodations when they arrived. Then came the **Great Depression** (1929 – 1939), considered the worst economic downturn in the industrial period, resulting in the stock market crash and panic on Wall Street. The stock market crash wiped out millions of investors. African Americans were the first to be fired and last to be hired. It should be no surprise that Marcus Garvey emerged and formed the Universal Negro Improvement Association (UNIA) to encourage Black people to build a nation in Africa of their own making; a campaign called the "Back to Africa" movement.

On the other end of the spectrum, scholar, W.E.B DuBois was outspoken about the civil rights of Blacks throughout the world and formed the National Association for the Advancement of Colored People (NAACP). DuBois and Booker T. Washington were on public record as they argued to define the role of Black people in America. Despite their efforts, history shows, Black people remained economically impoverished and politically powerless. Even DuBois, after years of trying to help Black people overcome, moved to Ghana until his death. During **World War II** (1939-1945), gave an economic and psychological boost to African Americans, as they were hired and trained to perform high-paying jobs since most White people were engulfed in the war efforts. The Servicemen Readjustment Act of 1944, administered between 1944-1949 provided nearly 9 million veterans to receive $4 billion from the bill's unemployment compensation program. For those 125,000 Blacks who served in combat did so in all-Black units (approximately 6.25% of all forces) were denied access to the GI bill. While some Blacks served as mess hall attendants and cooks, the military gave Blacks an opportunity to rise in rank to be aviators, like the famous Tuskegee Airman and Naval Officers. By 1942, the United States Marine Corp (USMC) started to recruit African Americans in all-Black units. Inventors, like Henrietta Bradberry, developed a Torpedo Discharging mechanism that enabled torpedoes to be fired while submerged in water. Dr. Charles Drew was a surgeon who developed a technique for storing large-scale blood banks during WWII. While African Americans took advantage of their opportunities afforded them by the military, back home many Blacks still lived under the shadow of Jim Crow laws and were forced to use separate public establishments and facilities. To avoid another depression, the U.S. Government passed the GI Bill of Rights honoring the greatest generation veterans who served in the war with a college education, making up fifty percent of college admissions. The bill provided for tuition, books, and supplies, counseling services, and living allowance. The bill was discriminatory, as it was administered during Jim Crow laws and did not accommodate African Americans. Despite unfair treatment for Black people, the number of African Americans serving in the military increased during the **Korean War** (1945-1953), where 600,000 served in the Pacific Campaign and nearly 5,000 were killed according to military estimates. One might say, this war provided the first real recognition by the United States for the contribution of African Americans serving the country with honor and distinction. On July 26, 1948, President Harry Truman (#33) signed an Executive Order to desegregate the armed forces. While this action by the president was monumental, African Americans could still not vote across the south and faced housing discrimination and segregated schools in the north. All the sacrifices made by the previous Black generations to be accepted by America were waning. Young people across the socio-economic spectrum were growing more impatient and intolerant of the U.S. Government. White liberals and Black radicals were critical of American aggression in the world. It took the US Supreme Court nearly 58 years since "Plessy v. Ferguson", to reverse the decision in 1954, in "Brown versus the Board of Education", making it illegal to separate public facilities based on race. The United States found itself entering another military conflict, as the outcry of the American people was split why the nation was entering into yet another war. During the transition of power from President Dwight Eisenhower (#34) to President John F. Kennedy (#35), the U.S. Government became involved in the **Vietnam War** (1961-1975). According to historical doctrine was because the United States feared the expansion of Communism. After 19 years, the U.S. was unable to defeat the Vietcong, including the Laotian Civil War, and Cambodia. By 1975, all three countries officially declared themselves Communist. Interesting enough, African Americans played a prominent role in Vietnam. A total of 300,000 African Americans served in the Vietnam War (forty percent) of all draftees. African Americans made up a significant portion of the combat units (twenty-three percent), and forty-five to sixty percent of airborne troops were African Americans. The U.S. Navy had the fewest African Americans in this campaign. American media sentiment for the war dogged the country's involvement, as anti-war protest movement amongst students spilled over into the Black community. Because of racism at home added fuel to tension resulted in civil disorder across the country where major riots erupted in large urban cities. Black people seized the opportunity to callout discrimination against the government for using Blacks in disproportional numbers during the war efforts. During the **Civil Rights Movement**, African Americans worked tirelessly to end racial discrimination and gain equal rights under the law. Amid the Vietnam War, the **Civil Rights Act** (1964) passed legislation prohibiting discrimination based on race, color, religion, sex, or national origin. Further, the act forbade discrimination as it related to race and sex in hiring, promoting, and firing. The Civil Rights Movement eventually led to action. For example, Thurgood Marshall became the first African American Supreme Court justice, appointed by President Lyndon B. Johnson (#36), to the Supreme Court of the United States (SCOTUS) in June 1967, and confirmed by Senate with a vote of 69 to 11.

Mr. Marshall was a strong advocate of racial equality during the early movement and argued 32 cases before the SCOTUS where he won 29 of those cases. Most people are aware of the non-violent civil rights leader, Rev. Martin Luther King, Jr., who came out of the Southern Christian Leadership Conference and his antagonist, Malcom X, who came out of the Nation of Islam (NOI), argued for racial justice by any means necessary. This period in African American history, produced Affirmative Action to appease middle-class Blacks. Because the program was perceived as a quota system, it did very little to address the disfranchised Black community and angered White Americans. As a result, activist groups like the Black Panthers emerged to fill the gap to feed poor people and provide protection to the community. Upon the assassinations of King and Malcom X created a leadership vacuum giving rise to Minister Louis Farrakhan, who emerged with his controversial political views and charismatic rhetorical style, was supported by the military wing of the NOI. It was called the Fruit of Islam (F.O.I.). He was often praised by some Black people for trying to promote Black self-determination through economic development but criticized by mainstream media as an anti-Semitic. This is another example where Black people lacked control to propagate its own narrative and were therefore subjected to a powerful outside media view that divided African Americans because they feared economic and political retribution. As some Black people attempted to assimilate with its White American brethren, required adherence to political party talking points, continuing to stratify African American between the haves and have nots amongst them.

Unfair practices by creditors forced the government to pass the **Truth in Lending Act** (1968) to protect citizens against inaccurate and unfair credit billing. The act required lenders to provide cost of loan information so people could compare various loan options. As African American acquired the ability to secure consumer credit loans and credit cards, they were often placed in high-risk loans with higher interest rates compared to loans for White Americans, as historical records showed were skewed disproportionately against them. This structural framework set the groundwork to perpetuate a wealth gap in America. It was attorney, Charles Lewis Nier, III, who studied the effect of economic discrimination and brought to light how this Act did little to produce relief for Black people. And because African Americans had no political influence and lacked cohesion amongst the Black community could not impose any real pressure on lenders, causing the wealth gap between Whites and Blacks to expand. President Richard Nixon (#37) became president after his second attempt, losing to President Kennedy in 1960. The Nixon Administration produced two major milestones for the United States; one, he was instrumental in successfully opening new markets in China and expanding capitalism deep into Asia, and two, his administration was responsible for creating the Environmental Protection Agency (EPA) designed to protect the country from all forms of environmental pollution. Because President Nixon was an unpopular politician, his campaign had to rely on racist dog whistles to divide voters along racial lines in his re-election bid, and he won! Unfortunately, the Nixon Administration became under siege for the cover-up charges that ended his presidency in disgraced and subsequent impeachment amid the Watergate scandal. African Americans continued to protest to no avail, and despite overt discrimination, rose to dominance in areas of individual athletics and entertainment throughout the world. Their communities were devastated by Heroin and other illicit drugs. Blacks lesser-known contributions to American innovation are rarely mentioned, like Physicist, George Carruthers, in 1972, invented the Ultraviolet Camera-Spectrograph for the NASA Apollo 16 mission. Unfortunately, he was rare because African Americans lacked access to quality post-high school education, so many continued to enlist in the armed services due to few options. The **U.S. Conflict in the Middle East** (1974) dates back centuries of Western involvement in the region. The U.S. government installed two puppet leaders in Iran and Iraq. Beginning with the Shah of Iran, Mohammed Reza Pahlavi, who ruled from 1941 - 1979, and later, installed Saddam Hussein, President of Iraq, from 1979 - 2003. The United States had a vested interest in controlling the massive oil reserves. The U.S. presence in the region continued under President Gerald Ford (#38). Over the next three decades, the rich and powerful on Wall Street would continue to manipulate U.S. economic policies by manufacturing financial schemes that caused cyclical recessions that produced winners and losers.

And people of color were amongst the biggest losers of them all. Over time, the country would see a massive transfer of wealth going to one percent of the wealthiest people in America. Under President Jimmy Carter (#39); who was perceived as weak in domestic and foreign policies, the nation plunged into a deep recession known as **Stagflation** (1980**)** resulting in high oil prices and high unemployment.

According to Keynesian economist, stagnation is when there is slow economic growth occurring simultaneously with high rates of inflation. High inflation is a decline in purchasing power of a currency, and therefore, no value in saving money. Wall Street continued to control the winners and losers, causing the stock market to fall twenty percent in a single day on October 19, 1987. A precursor of the event lay with the use of a computer program software model to adjust monetary and foreign trade agreements to manipulate U.S currency, including insurance instruments led to **Black Monday** (1987). It was President Ronald Reagan (#40); a skillful politician, who also played the race card to influence White Americans to vote along racial lines, and was the first to use the slogan, "Make America Great Again", which devastated the poor, stripping the country of mental health care and dismantling labor unions. President George H.W. Bush (#41), Reagon's Vice President became under siege as a result of the draconian tax cut from the Reagan Era was forced to raise taxes against his promise to help the country recover. Bush (#41) lost his bid for re-election. Before leaving office, he led a successful military campaign with the **Gulf War** (1990). Unfortunately, the war disproportionally enlisted African Americans in the U.S. Army, and they paid a heavy price, making up fifteen percent of combat troops during earliest part of conflict resulting in the highest causalities. The country experienced economic expansion under President Bill Clinton (#42) driven by the emergence of e-Commerce, producing winners like eBay, Amazon, and Google between 1995-2000. There was a slight economic downturn related to the **Tech Bubble** (2000) where combined companies lost $1.77 trillion or seventy-five percent of its value when the stock market speculation crashed due to the weakening internet-based business model. It was under this popular Democratic president that enacted 1994 Federal Crime Bill, which incentivize states to build prisons and incarcerate more people than any other country in the world, and disproportionally more African Americans. Under President George W. Bush (#43), the country experienced great unrest. Bush (#43) extended his father's Gulf War as part of his so-called Axis of Evil agenda, referring to Muammar Gadhafi of Libya, Kim Jong-Un of North Korea, and Saddam Hussein of Iraq. His Administration fabricated the weapons of mass destruction stemming from 9/11 attack on the World Trade Center. U.S. Forces also occupied Afghanistan, Syria, and other Middle Eastern countries. The real damaged occurred during the **Real Estate Bust** of 2007 that disproportionately affected Blacks and Latino borrowers. Dating back to the Clinton Administration, efforts to facilitate more homeownership amongst Blacks and Latinos was a priority. These groups received high-cost, high-risk mortgage loans with variable rates based on faulty high appraisal value to embellish credit worthiness. Operatives on Wall Street converted these sub-prime loans into attractive investment packages called derivatives and sold them around the world but eventually the loans were defaulted on leading to the collapse of Lehman Brothers and other financiers. Their collapse triggered a global crash that led to the **Great Recession** (2008). The Great Recession (2009-2013) lingered well into the presidency of President Barrack Obama (#44). He spent most of his first term securing a safety net for many Americans without health care, and enacted into law, the **Affordable Healthcare Act – ACA** (2010). Ironically, the ACA helped more poor White people than people of color because of the legislative control in Red States governed by Republicans did little to benefit Black people who lived in those states.

POST-AFRICAN AMERICAN SLAVERY

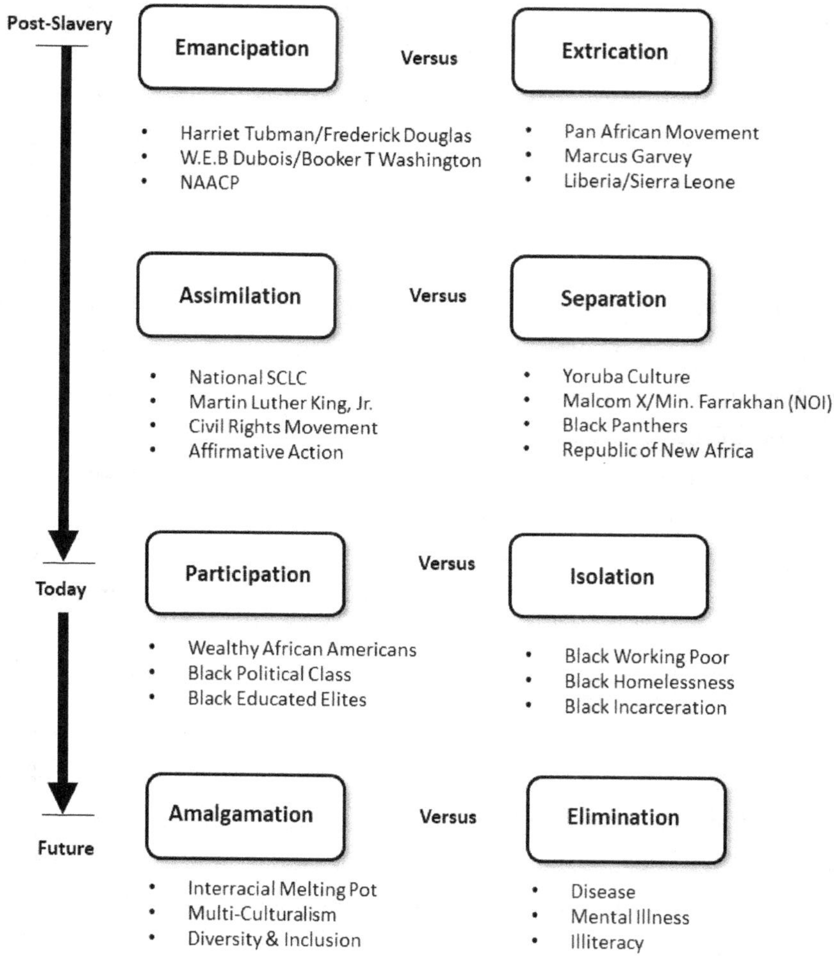

By the end of Obama's second term, which ended in 2016, the country was recovering from the recession; strides were made with Human Rights, Gay Rights, and third-world nations allowed women access to education; yet black people in the U.S. continued to fall behind. The **Coronavirus Pandemic (COVID-19)** shutdown of the world economy in 2020 exposed the United States racist tendencies that plagued the country since its inception, where limited job opportunities forged conflicts between poor Whites and working-class Blacks. The Far-right fringe operatives comprised of

White nationalist, White supremacist, and Q-Anon conspiracy groups exacerbated the resentment and divisiveness along racial lines. President Donald A. Trump (#45) took the country by storm, often aligned with White Nationalist and White Supremacist sympathizers, as he recycled President Reagan's old slogan, "Make America Great Again". President Trump was relentless when it came to confronting and streamlining government bureaucracy, and established a new branch of the armed forces, called the U.S. Space Force. His Administration pushed scientist to initiate Operation Warp Speed to rapidly develop a vaccine for the coronavirus. However, his miscalculation of managing the COVID-19 pandemic and unhinged behavior cost him a second term. He lost the popular vote, and the Electoral College vote, (306 versus 232) to President-Elect, Joe Biden (#46). Too much amaze, President Trump increased the number of Black male voters to his side. The Trump presidency and subsequent 2020 Presidential Election changed the political landscape in American governance. The political divide amongst White conservatives and White liberals left the country unrecognizable. One can see with their own eyes how wealth, political power, and misinformation, and an alternative reality can sway people to vote against their own best interest. One could say there has been lots of progress for Black people, because after all, they are no longer legally beaten to death in public, humiliated and shackled in prison camps like they were during slavery, Hmmm? It should be painfully clear that most Black people do not enjoy the America dream. In fact, not once during the chronicle of African American history could a zenith period be sighted, where the slogan, "Make America Great Again", had any real meaning for African Americans. There is about 328,000,000 people living in the United States, with Black people making up twelve percent of the population according to the U.S. Census. Black people still rank at the bottom of demographical statistics regarding wealth and education compared to other groups. There are 607 billionaires in the U.S., and seven Black people are billionaires. There are one in seven White families defined as millionaires or fifteen percent of all millionaires, compared to one in 50 for Black families or two percent of all millionaires. According to the U.S. Census data,

26 million Black people or sixty percent of its population is considered middle-class; people who earn between $23,000-$25,000 per year. **The Inflation Reduction Act** (2021) is another example how monetary policymakers are impacting the American people. The government pumped billions of dollars into the U.S. economy to artificially prop up various industries, and now we need a plan to combat an impending inflation on the horizon that will disproportionally affect poor families.

THE AFRICAN AMERICAN UNIFICATION DILEMMA

According to some Constantine Christian religious theologians, suggested the Negroid came from the second son of Noah, named Ham. Supposedly the descendants of Ham are Cush, Egypt (Mizraim), Put, and Canaan. Some paleontologist and scientist concluded African people populated the entire continent of Africa, creating civilizations from Egypt to Mozambique. Before the Persian and European Conquests, all of Egypt and modern Sudan, was occupied by Nubians. From the Golden Age of Ancient Egypt to the African Empires of the Middle Ages (e.g., Mali, Songhay, and Ghana), African people were always diverse in customs, language, religion, physical appearance, and technological advancement, but always connected by land.

According to the Five Gate Theory, it lists the reasons for the fall of African empires: 1) Lack of organizing diversity amongst the vast African nations, 2) Global desire for natural resources of African nations, including human trafficking, 3) Climate change, via the desertification led to the migration from North Africa, 4) Human errors related to the naivety, as African leaders assumed and accepted outsiders as equal in morals choosing to forgive rather than oppose them, and 5) Muslim and Christian religious missionaries.

The eventual fall of African empires and their long-standing influence over the ancient world came to an end when they were supplanted by the Persian Empire who militarized African soldiers known as the Moors to expand Islam. With the help of African Moors and Arab Moors invaded Spain and colonized much of northern Africa, including Egypt, Libya, Algeria, and Morocco. By the 1900's, seven European powers (Britain, France, Germany, Belgium, Spain, Portugal, and Italy) systematically carved up and colonized the African continent except for Ethiopia and Libya. Most African slaves transported to the Americas came from the Senegal, Mali, and Gambia Rivers region, including what is now called Angola and the Congo. The Portuguese began to kidnap African people, and later formed agreements with British middlemen to produce the Trans-Atlantic Slave Trade Industry to distribute African slaves to the new world. Of all the European powers, Britain was the most successful, as the legacy of their colonies still exist and flourish today, namely the United States of America. As examined from the Chronicle of African Americans, the intermixing of African slaves further divided those African tribes who originally lived along the western coast of the Africa. Many slave owners further complicated the likelihood that such a disjointed collection of African diaspora could unite under a common bond, given the miscegenation of the African female slaves. But that is exactly what the foundation is attempting to accomplish. The foundation used here is a philosophical term used to describe the basis for all other things to be built upon it.

The foundation must be instrumental in drafting acceptable reparation language amongst Americans to ensure we address the government's role in the enslavement of African people and the prolonged systemic social injustices against their descendants. The first provision calls for an African American Reparations Act of 2030 to be administered through an African American Infrastructure Bill. While there are many foundations supported by Black people; everything from the arts to other philanthropic causes, the foundation wants to embrace them all as part of the building blocks to unify under a single umbrella. The universal meaning pertains to the unification of African Americans as a whole, body and thought. Let's address a couple of points of clarification; first, the foundation is not a trade organization or legal activist group, nor should it be confused with an economic development advocacy program for distressed urban communities.

While it will encompass a lobbying arm like the American Economic Institute, the Heritage Foundation and the Brookings Institute, a better resemblance would be more like, the Wakanda Council, of the fictional Marvel Comics movie, Black Panther, as an attempt to unite the various tribes (various factions of African Americans). The basis of the foundation serves as a microcosm to collect and act upon diverse opinions, but still fosters a spirit of unification and reconciliation. African American reparations will only come by way of energizing entrepreneurship amongst its people in a way never achieved in modern history. The African American Infrastructure Bill will serve as a catalyst and enable African Americans to remake the Tulsa, Oklahoma model better than before. The "strategic roadmap" would not be complete without a legal contract with the United States that establishes a financial agreement with African Americans to implement large-scale infrastructure projects in parts of the country. The African American Infrastructure Bill will serve as the framework for the reparations, containing two important provisions. One makes up an economic provision designed to accelerate access into unchartered industries and markets, and the second includes a regulatory and social justice provisions designed to provide Black people immediate access to education, training and investment that incentivizes upward mobility through community development.

The communities of modern-day African America are complex and non-monolithic. The assumption of a one-size fits all approach will not work, and therefore, the foundation must define some guiding principles to include the gamut of Black people into a truly organic conversation to prepare a cohesive plan acceptable to most of the American people. The foundation must devise a diversity campaign of its own making to display for the entire world to see. Imagine if African Americans could rise from one of the most oppressive conditions of mankind (slavery) and bring global recognition to its people. The foundation must leverage its greatest asset, the Black woman. We can see the impact of grassroots Black sorority organizations emerge with unprecedented political clout in the United States. Black men must not resist the influence of the Black woman, as Western culture has changed the paradigm of Nubian nation hierarchy. Historically, it was commonplace for Black woman to hold positions of leadership and power, to the extent that Nubia was viewed as an empire ruled by women. We saw strong women from the early Suffragette Movement in the United States, where Black woman were active participants, like Sojourner Truth, Harriet Tubman, Frances Ellen Watkins, and Fannie Lou Hamer. Modern Black women like Sherilynn Infill, from the NAACP legal defense fund who continues to fight for social injustice and equality is a great example. And let's not forget, it was Stacy Abrams, former Georgia State House of Representative, who made all the difference in the 2020 Presidential election that changed the political landscape across the U.S. and in the State of Georgia. In western culture, here and now, Black woman must be mindful and considerate of the Black man roles, and avoid emasculating them, but rather lifting them up to reach their full potential.

The foundation must create an environment beyond the two-party systems to forge a debate to determine new alliances and design separate, but complementary platforms widely communicated to the African American masses for consumption. For example, a conservative platform will want to pull back regressive taxation, while a liberal platform might call for more human services to support the poor. Regardless of the political party, the distribution curve must ensure that the needs are met for the small percent of high-income earners and poor-income earners, while balancing engagement with the larger percent of the middle-income population.

The foundation must embrace interdenominational faith to serve the entire Black community, which includes African-decent immigrants. For example, these immigrants make up one-fifth of the U.S. Muslim population, while African Americans who make up twelve percent of the U.S. population predominantly (seventy-nine percent) belongs to some form of Christianity, and only two percent are Muslim. The remaining African American population do not identify with any religion. The enlightened clergy must broaden the teachings of the Black church to educate their flock to accept the secular population supported by the foundation without compromising their individual religious doctrines. While the foundation is not about dictating social norms, the foundation must be comfortable with upholding the Second Amendment Right to Bear Arms, and Roe V. Wade, and supporting the Lesbian, Gay, Bisexual, Transsexual, and Queer (LGBTQ) community. A lack of support for these civil rights could risk being viewed as discriminatory, out of touch, and alienating segments of the Black population.

The foundation must come to terms with its own narrative; both within the Black community and how people perceive African Americans around the world. The foundation must overcome four challenges to unify black people in America: 1) relieve the economic constraints amongst the population; 2) resolve the social differences amongst the population, 3) provide education reform needed to raise the aptitude of the population, and 4) create an African American narrative to facilitate an environment for interdenominational religions to co-exist and thrive.

Even more daunting, is it will face challenges from certain American factions who will oppose any form of reparations, causing conflicts and maintaining barriers to prevent Black people entry into certain industries. Some quarters may see the foundation as a new attempt to break away from the U.S. government to form a provisional government within its border, which is far from the truth. What is true is the desire to establish a Basecamp for African Americans; a concentration of landownership and center of global commerce, a brain trust of innovative technology, and the ability to set political policies and deploy favorable messaging to the world audiences. The complexities involved are real, but if the terms and conditions are appropriately crafted, each obstacle has a potential solution. The economic constraint is tied to the distribution of natural resources. The foundation must help determine the equitable transfer of natural resources through economic and community development investment initiatives that focus on an education and job training pipeline. The social differences are divided amongst religious and secular norms, which include a need for rapid education reform, community outreach and engagement. For example, if people are educated and productive, reduces idle time amongst inner-city youth and young adults reducing the likelihood of violent crimes against its own people. If the youth and young adults' efforts are redirected towards achievable goals, where their basic needs are satisfied (food, clothing, and shelter), will shift behaviors from negativism and hopelessness towards positive thoughts of social movement (sense of belonging) and self-esteem (sense of accomplishment). It is here where the African American narrative takes shapes and enlightened Black people can mobilize the social movement towards unification. If African Americans can mount a movement to facilitate an environment for religious reconciliation amongst African American Christians, Muslims and other religions practiced across the gamut of Black people is beneficial. Until there is some kind of consensus amongst African Americans, any sort of genuine reparations will not be successful. And, left to the U.S. government alone will be deliberately slow and will most likely produce what amounts to an antiquated policy by the time any real amendments are passed by Congress.

THE GAMUT OF AFRICAN AMERICAN DIVERSITY

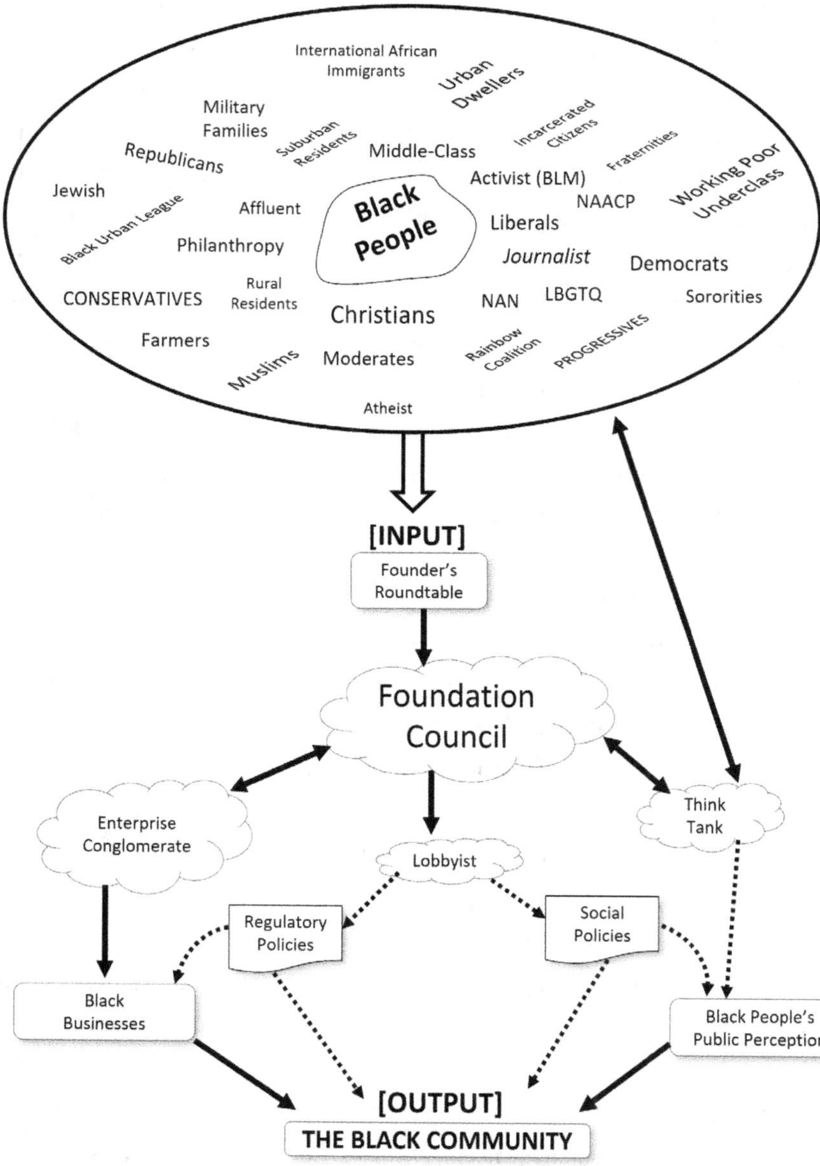

The masses of Black people were divided and conquered well before the Emancipation Proclamation. They were torn apart literally by whippings, separated from their languages and families by physically moving family members' miles apart from one another to work the fields amongst other lost souls, and psychologically tortured, diminishing their self-worth as human beings. By the time African slaves won their legal freedom, they were way behind the learning curve as to how they would survive and navigate their journey in the new world. The shortcomings fall into three fundamental pillars that never aligned for black people: 1) Economic Empowerment; 2) Political Influence, and 3) the ability to shape their own narrative and social norms. The inability to organize trustworthy institutions amongst themselves gave way to paltry institutions as the divisions can be seen played out throughout the chronicle of African American history. Opposing views started immediately, between the Emancipation versus Extrication Period, opposing arguments of whether to stay in America or go back to Africa. Even amongst the emancipated Black people, intense debate took place about the appropriate role, occupation, and career path of the Negro. Despite having their legal freedom in hand, early freed Blacks lacked economic power, many ex-slaves lost their property, or had it stripped away because they had very little political power to fight back, especially since they were not allowed to vote. The family structure became the basis for shaping young people, as the elders could only provide encouragement to their kids to dream big.

As seen during the Assimilation versus Separation Period, Black people were still divided. The Black families who managed to educate their children pressed on for equality as they made their way into the middle-income classification, albeit at lower wages, than their White contemporaries. On the one hand, the Blacks who remained poor found themselves on the outside and disenfranchised. Today, Black males experienced the highest incarceration rate in the U.S., which devastated Black families and single mothers were forced to raise children alone, causing a breakdown of the fragile Black family unit. Some African Americans became more radicalize and sought to create a separate society within the United States. Just as generations before them, Black people of this era failed to create a concentration of wealth. Conversely, it was during the Assimilation versus Separatist period where Blacks made significant inroads in political office and military ranks, via Affirmative Action legislation. However, Blacks lost the battle when it came to shaping their own narrative. The nuclear family structure destroyed what little influence the family had on shaping the minds of their children. The powerful imagery of television, movies and music reprogrammed the entire race to see them through the lens of others. And now Blacks find themselves in a period of the participation versus isolation, and despite the vast wealth of high-profile African Americans, and a strong political presence in the Democratic Party, young Black people still see themselves assigned to stereotypes made up of criminals, rappers, athletes, and political sellouts. The most powerful tool available (social media) is under the control of others. Keep in mind, throughout all the previously mentioned periods, there were always wealthy Black people who rose to the top of the sports and entertainment industry. Now, Black people must find a new way to consolidate its wealth to seize political clout in a way that mandates the inclusion of African Americans into the fabric of American society.

Early colonial biracial people came about from miscegenation, a term originating in 1864, referring to the blending of the races when slave owners raped African slave woman producing mulatto offsprings. During the early writings of President Thomas Jefferson, he condoned this practice, and many White people espoused his point of view. Even prior to his presidency (1801 – 1809), the mindset was to breed the black out of the African to improve them and make them more acceptable. And over time, Americans adopted the British colonialism model used in China and India, favoring lighter skin as more desirable. Black Americans adopted the thinking as well.

In addition to the historical miscegenation, today, African Americans are made up of biracial people resulting from interracial sexual relations and marriages between many different ethnicities. In the meantime, it has not been helpful to continuously perpetuate this false narrative in the media. Here we are in 2022, and a lack of control over its own media continuously sees darker African Americans portrayed as marginalized.

Today, powerful media moguls are communicating their vision and shaping the narrative, as you can see there is still a mindset who believes we could breed the blackness out of African Americans to make them more acceptable. A large segment of progressives who support African American causes, like voter's rights, human rights, civil rights, and Black Lives Matter, still foster a victim-minded approach to saving Black people and to help them cope with the established power structure, but not necessarily ready to relinquish their own White privilege.

We can see the racial amalgamation play out in movies and commercials through subliminal messages of interracial harmony to show a less threatening and more acceptable portrayal of Black people. This redefining of blackness in America is the strongest argument why it will be difficult to pursue reparations. Because of interracial marriages and, African Americans tendency to identify as multicultural, and not Black could seriously challenge African American reparations with the American people.

DEFINING AFRICAN AMERICAN BLACKNESS

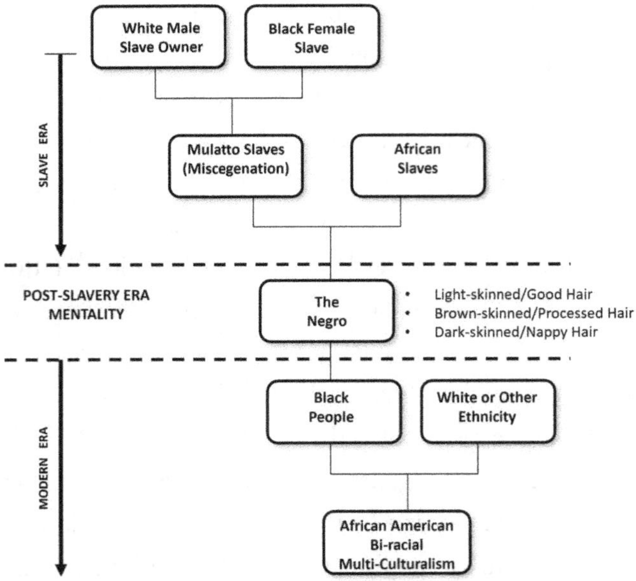

While it is a fact that African Americans are composed of mixed races, as many people are, including some White people. The reinforcement of "identity politics" amongst the progressive is not helpful. The vice president of the United States, Kamala Harris, who serves with President Joe Biden, is noted for being the first Asian-African American woman to serve in the office, a desired characteristic.

Adding to the complexity is the wealthy progressive-minded Black persons, perhaps knowingly or unknowingly is complicit, as they attempt to overlay images of idealistic bohemian afro-centric culture that is completely devoid of any real connection to the experiences of most Black people living in America. What makes matters worse, popular musicians and entertainers reinforce Black stereotypes, often depicting Black people as backwards thinking and inarticulate people who will bring your property value down when they move into your neighborhoods. In pursuit of their personal financial gain, fosters an egregious injustice of false narrative against their own people. I understand their point for survival, but the measure of success or failure depends on your perspective.

If social and racial harmony amongst the American people is achieved, it could diminish future talks of reparation. An increase in multiculturalism could lead to an indigenous people like status. The amalgamation of Black people would be complete, and the narrative of American history would be validated, as descendants of the African American slave would have reached social equilibrium, but perhaps not as the Rev. Dr. Martin Luther King, Jr. envisioned. It took 156 years since, June 19, 1865 (aka, Juneteenth), marking the official end of slavery in the United States of America, that President Biden, decreed Juneteenth to be a federal holiday.

Reconciliation

- Economic Consolidation
- Political Cooperation
- Narrative Orchestration

It is ironic, given the background surrounding the holiday, disenfranchised Black people find themselves at the bottom of the wealth gap, limited political influence and depicted as a drag on society. Throughout American history, Blacks have not found a way to consolidate their resources to influence the system to work for them. Imagine if even a small portion of the estimated $1.1 trillion in African American spending power remained in Black neighborhoods what a difference it could make to improve people's lives if managed properly. The fact of the matter, money flows into Black neighborhoods, and very little exchanges hands or is reinvested back into the neighborhood.

If the course of Black history is to change, the foundation must reverse the defective mitosis within the African American mindset and mend the divisiveness between Americans by promoting reconciliation. A higher level of thought is required to find ways to create wealth that will enable Black people to influence legislatures to change laws that will benefit people of color. Also, developing an image how the rest of the world will view African

American businesses, brands, products, and services. A new African American narrative is an essential part of the process. Without a new social compass, Black people will be no better off than they are today.

A large part of American morals are degenerating, taking the proportionally smaller groups, like African Americans down with it. The decision facing Black people is to stay the status quo of disillusionment and witness the weakest amongst them fall by the wayside, or will enlightened Black people rise up to confront the shadows of colonialism and revive its people? The idea of racial segregation is like dividing up a box of wax crayons. They are all the same compositionally but provide distinctions of varying strips. It is a human flaw and destructive nature of social engineering that assign hierarchy based on the color of one's skin.

THREE-DIMENSIONAL SOCIAL CONSTRUCT OF AFRICAN AMERICANS

Even colonialism could not purge out the basic tenets of Black people from their ancestry, as they identify with people of African descent. Even though most poor to middle-income African Americans are amongst the lowest educated, they are amongst the most conservative people in the United States, making the cultivation of relationships with progressives and liberal thinkers challenging to reconcile.

If the process of racial intermixing continues and predominate the African American identity, the more appropriate term is Amalgamation. In America, a successful ethnic group is measured on a per capita basis by U.S. Census data that tabularizes their contribution to the country's GDP. Throughout African American history, the only constants are poverty and discrimination, legislative bias, and mass incarceration. As previously highlighted in the African American chronicle, self-determination and self-reliance were always opposed. The foundation must understand how to reinvent the social construct of persuasion that promotes new institutional processes and systems that will ensure future generational leaders can succeed. It is imperative to garner support to sustain economic power and political influence, as well as framing a new narrative for Black people. It should be noted that without the support of good-hearted principled White people, the progress of African Americans, albeit slow, would not exist.

On the opposite end of the spectrum, a certain segment of White people will always default to fear because they believe Black people are non-Americans who only seek revenge for American slavery. To be clear, the foundation wants to build economic power for African Americans, so they can live and pursue happiness and decide how they are viewed by the world. The objective of the MEAC is to foster a collaborative breakthrough understanding about what it will take to build a tangible multi-cultural Black community along with other groups in America. It is great to witness the success of individual African Americans, but they alone, operating as a singular entity, separate and apart of any concerted plan to engage the masses of Black people is meaningless to the cause. And only they can decide if they want to assume a role.

It is important to note, without all the voices working together to advocate for a solution would continue the slow progress of making America a more perfect union. In the final analysis, African Americans must be smarter. The process of social change must be set up strategically. It should be common knowledge that relying on individualism, the status quo of political conformity and random social activism and disruptive civil disorder will not produce real change. Only a well-planned and deliberate social movement of the American people thinking in the same way will produce a real change for good. The progressive solution of welfare, imprisonment and propagating false narratives of victimization has not, nor will not correct the sins of American Slavery. Moreover, it will only worsen and prolong institutional racism and disenfranchisement for Black people in the long run. Until Black people are allowed to participate in the American experiment fully, America will never overcome the shadows of its past. Throughout history, civilizations have always tried to control the world, as the human obsession with riches and power has never proven sustainable, nor will it be in the future. It doesn't mean that people will stop trying, as we see with the nexus of space exploration. While African Americans are preoccupied with social justice, other nations are working on man-made space habitats. The elites and the very wealthy are punching their tickets to reserve a place in the new frontier, while poor people, and people of color are left behind to live in squalor in an environment of climate change and global warming; the ultimate juxtaposition between the "haves" and "have nots." At the same time, these same elites are educating and preparing their children to lead future voyages to pioneer new markets, whether on earth or in space. If African Americans continue its reliance on the government alone, it will not end well for Black people. The evolution of great empires always seems to emerge, accompanied by knowledge of science, control of natural resources, and the ability to solve problems through technology. Will African Americans help America remain a country of opportunity?

THE ENTERPRISE

Throughout the history of the United States, African Americans played a role influencing science and medicine, politics, and legislation, becoming captains of industry and leading multi-national corporations. And more recently, its branding of sports and entertainment pop culture trends across the globe.

Despite great achievements, African Americans continue to lag behind other ethnic groups when it comes to creating wealth, which diminishes its ability to determine the destiny of their communities. According to a U.S. Economy & News report, slavery legally prevented Black people from building wealth until the 13th Amendment in 1865. The practice continued under Jim Crow laws well into the late 1950s. The idea of Black Americans utilizing principles of capitalism is not a new concept. Dating back to 1895, where so-called New Negroes were described in an article of the Cleveland Gazette, suggesting that educated Black people emerged from post-Civil War with money and political influence developed their own communities through self-help and racial pride. Well-known leaders like Booker T. Washington, W.E.B. DuBois, and Alexander Crumwell were instrumental in producing many successful institutions during their era.

Over the past five decades, the wealth gap between Whites and Blacks has increased. Another study reported in the Atlantic, stated African Americans are uncomfortable talking about their holdings, often using careers, homes, and other status symbols rather than actual wealth barometers. A consolidation of wealth is the impetus that will enable African Americans to assume a controlling interest of national institutions, major sport teams and entertainment platforms to overcome the challenge of unification and economic transformation for future Black generations.

THE ENENTERPRISE

PREFACE

The purpose of the enterprise is to target wealthy Black people to espouse the plan contain herein to change the trajectory of Black wealth in the U.S. I prepared this paper with wealthy African Americans in mind, in the hopes of persuading them to form a new consciousness. I want to engage people of means to help amass substantial holdings to acquire, manage, and grow multiple market segments, via a conglomerate enterprise. It was essential in the previous paper to point out issues before achieving this financial milestone. There is no hiding from the facts that the complexities of these differences are real and have given way to Black people's fragmented state. The goal of the Manifesto of Emerging American Capitalism (MEAC) is to build a national economic power base by assembling capital, natural resources, talent, and expertise capable of forming a new business enterprise comprised primarily of African Americans stakeholders. I examined successful economic growth models from India, Korea, and Japan. The Korean and Japanese models are closer to the goals and objectives selected for the foundation with some cultural difference. In general, the Korean model, called "Chaebol", is based on an internal collective (Family Centered), for example, companies like Samsung, LG, Hyundai, and SK are owned by wealthy families. The Japanese model, called "Keiretsu", is based on an external collective (Society Centered), for example, the original members included Mitsui, Mitsubishi, Fuyo, Sanwa, and Dialchi Kangyo Bank (DKB). Let's begin with some operational definitions to level set a common understanding.

The United States is a Republic system of government with a democracy ideology. As a republic, the U.S. is made up of 50 individual states unified under a set of declarations. Each state is entitled to elect the unifying office of the President of the United States under the Electoral College system. The electoral system is based on the number of U.S. Senators (100) and U.S. Congressional Districts (438), with a total 538 possible congressional officers. In theory, our democracy ideology suggests that when most state members vote, the electoral vote affirms the popular vote of that state. The Union was developed by wealthy people of the Planter class who had designed the system to ensure continuity and political power. The framers designed it so that only a third of the U.S. Senate could turnover for any given election cycle to ensure stability between new governments. While the U.S. Census is supposed to address shifts in demographics across the country, in practice, the U.S. congressional districts are redlined to ensure bias so that one political party would maintain control. To appreciate the simple elegance of the American franchise, one must distinguish between U.S. rules of constitutional law, and U.S. branding and marketing. America embraced the theories of Adam Smith, often referred to as the first theorist of capitalism. While Smith never used the term "capitalism," it was widely used in the late nineteenth century to describe a commercial society. America has never veered away from its capitalistic roots, and as a result, created the wealthiest concentration of people in modern history. On one hand, the society benefited from these industrial markets driven by innovation and technology because the advancements led to lengthening human life expectancy, raised the quality of life for everyday people and produced remarkable research and development beyond human imagination. On the other hand, history shows that pure capitalism is not about fairness, charity and equal portions, as imminent winners prevailed.

To ensure survival of the U.S. capitalist franchise, tweaks were required to keep the masses engaged, resulting in the European style; Mixed Economy (market-socialism system).

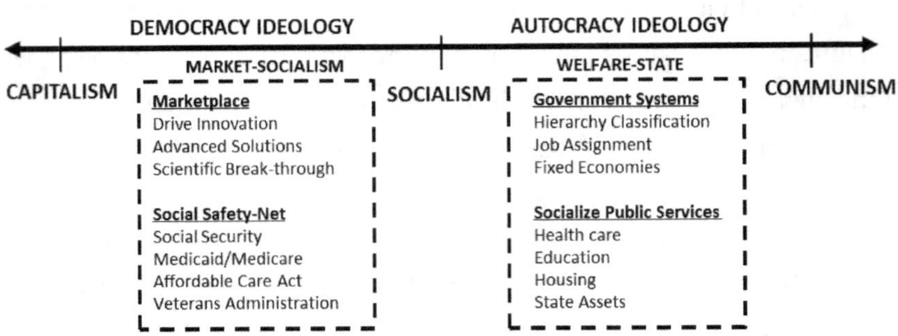

Americans, who reject the notion that the United States has no socialist overtures, are misguided. The U.S. budget (2015) is broken down into three categories: 1) <u>Mandatory Spending</u> represents sixty-five percent of the total budget; ($2.45 trillion went to Social Security, Unemployment and Labor), 2) Discretionary Spending represents twenty-nine percent of the total budget; ($1.11 trillion went to the Military Complex), and 3) Interest on Federal debt, represents six percent of the total budget, or $229 billion. Most countries throughout the world are moving closer to a market-socialist economy, where a few power players are driving new markets. The opening up of new markets in places like China, Africa and the Middle East has created an environment of global perceptions and stereotypes. Take for example, how various brands, products, and services are perceived around the world, impacting real prosperity of these nations.

Regardless of how the so-called African American community is defined, all available financial data suggest the group produces very little products and have the least number of firms as percent of its population. This has brought into question their spending power and the difficulty to compute the totality of African American wealth. Black people need a new breed of leaders who can provide providence and promote reconciliation of its wealth to better quantify the real potential of African Americans.

The difference between the U.S. founding fathers and the founder's roundtable introduced in the previous essay emphasizes a need for collaboration between Black woman and Black men to commit in crafting a new deal for African Americans. While these challenges represent real opportunities for Black entrepreneurs, the impending rewards will remain fleeting if the group is unable to organize serious players. Black people need real power brokers who can raise capital and form long-range planning horizons resulting in a new brand of gentrification to benefit struggling Black communities. African American businesspeople must defy the narratives defined by outsiders who only seek to deprive people of their right to thrive in America.

INTRODUCTION

The enterprise approach is different from other U.S. corporate business plans because it includes the involvement of the American people. Most of the information presented in this paper is vanilla and practiced by corporations around the world. The difference of this plan is it introduces a rubric specifically for African Americans. The notion of consolidating African American resources under a strategically coordinated conglomerate with the aim of transforming and harnessing Black wealth is unprecedented on a large scale. This paper calls upon aspiring Black capitalists to envision a system designed of its own making to effectively close the wealth gap and solve the poverty problem by elevating Black people and building a tangible Black community. The Manifesto of Emerging American Capitalism (MEAC) outlines a business management processes without all the unnecessary rhetoric and wordy explanations. Additionally, it offers a simple framework to organize a significant Black enterprise in America. The goal is to shift the paradigm from a singular minded business unit into a Black conglomerate structure to reimagine how people do business in America. African Americans must utilize the creativity and expertise of its best people to develop unimaginable products and services to generate wealth and influence. It begins with knowledgeable people who possess the integrity and vision to lead; people who understand the rules of engagement, having a business plan and access to capital. Strong leaders with a proven track record will enable the enterprise to attract investors, as well as leverage loans and bonds to innovate and expand. Because the competition in the global marketplace is high, reinforces the need for credible leaders with an exceptional business management acumen to lead the organization. Today, executive teams must be comprised of people knowledgeable of corporate law and acquisition, financial systems, and market analytics, as well as the ability to develop long-range strategic planning horizons. The emergence of new business ideas has always derived from value innovation and market disruptions. Regardless of the industry, there is no escape from the competition, which is constantly seeking ways to carve out unchartered opportunities by eliminating outdated products in exchange for higher valued goods and services at a significantly lower price. Black entrepreneurs must understand the needs of people and why people have these needs and desires. Answering these questions is critical. Imagine Black entrepreneurs providing these goods and services to the people and the way to deliver them. The markets around the world will continue to be shaped by technology and innovation. To ensure Black companies sustain its financial viability, the enterprise must develop and manage a diversified portfolio. The enterprise portfolio must include the allocation of capital to invest in advanced technologies, packaging mergers, and acquisitions capable of infrastructure construction and product development, and the ability to maximize working capital to operate, and drive the value chain of brands and services across many market sectors.

Implementing the complexities outlined in this chapter will require highly competent, knowledgeable business leaders capable of executing long-range strategies and tactical horizons. Modeled in part after the Japanese Keiretsu and on the scale and scope of American conglomerates like Black Rock and the Carlyle Group, with some religious overlap like the Koch Brothers, but with a caveat. Because African Americans are more of a hybrid group, the foundation must devise an approach to bridge the divide between African Americans religious norms and the secular Black populations to avoid any "purity test" that could bring unnecessary attention and intrude upon the anonymity of the foundation, its banking system, and the conglomerate ownership.

AFRICAN AMERICAN ADAPTATION OF THE JAPANESE KEIRETSU SYSTEM

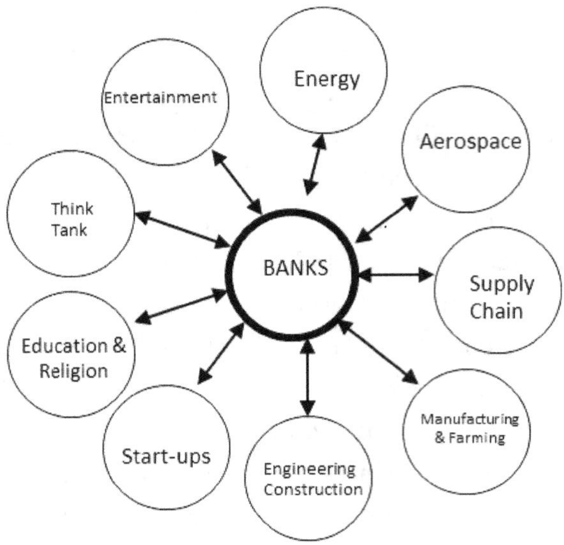

There are four strategic pillars of the African American Keiretsu (AAK), with each pillar playing a crucial role in establishing, developing, and maintaining the separation between religious virtues and private sector objectives.

The founder roundtable and conglomerate <u>owners</u> must govern the external African American collectives to become highly productive and contribute to the America's Gross Domestic Product (GDP) is a very significant and measurable manner.

THE PILLARS

<u>Pillar 1 – Foundation</u>: The founder's roundtable, made up, in part, of owners, who will devise the strategic plan with the board of directors for the parent company to advocate for causes important to African American interests. The foundation allows the free flow of ideas and interactions between principal parties to engage and strategize. It is under the foundation pillar where the emerging capitalist concept will take shape by forming the conglomerate enterprise. The foundation will facilitate potential investors and stakeholders to participate, as well as set the timeline and sequence of events.

<u>Pillar 2 – Leadership</u>: The "board of directors" is the head of the conglomerate, made up of owners and stakeholders who established the corporate governance standards and boundaries. The members of the board

are the primary owners and investors (private individuals and investment managers). The vision and mission of the board is to amass economic wealth and profitability for the enterprise to support initiatives that will enable the organization to accomplish its goals. The leadership must define its core values, as well as layout its organizational structure and identify the expertise needed to deliver results.

Pillar 3 – Management: The management team drives the vision, mission, and core value of the parent company. The "parent company" has oversight of capital to support the portfolio of brands and subsidiaries. The board of directors hires the chief executive officer (CEO) of the parent company. The CEO will hire highly educated people with exceptional business acumen. The goal and objective of the executive team is to deliver projected profits to the enterprise.

Pillar 4 – Operations: The "Brands and Subsidiaries" will operate as standalone businesses whose specific products and services will have global and niche market appeal. The vetted portfolio of companies will be acquired and institutionalized into the company's culture. The brands and subsidiaries are all about high-profit margin performance, utilizing lean methodologies and value innovation across every platform to eliminate waste and optimize profit, including the creation of high-value mainstream national brands and Afrocentric brands.

ESTABLISHING THE FOUNDATION

Pillar 1 – Foundation is a way to keep the MEAC evergreen between changes in leadership, which oversees a forum to bring like-minded African Americans together with a common goal of advancing an African American reparations and reconciliation agenda. The long-term goal of the foundation controls the AAK banking system to sustain African American interest. The near-term goal of the foundation is to establish the formation of the [Enterprise] ownership group.

This first pillar begins and ends with the same philosophical syllogism, which is the genesis of African American's ethical compass. To what extent are Black people willing to go to address social issues pertaining to healthcare, the impact of climate change and educating its workforce for an automated 21st Century. The foundation needs to consider a rebrand of social safety-nets as part of its value proposition to avoid conflating capitalist principles with social irresponsibility. To embrace capitalism in its purest sense is unrealistic. Society's reliance on communism, socialism, or capitalism alone tends to perform poorly. In the U.S., an exclusive capitalist system led to wealth inequalities at a disproportional level, producing a huge population of disenfranchised people. Western Europeans learned during the Ninetieth and Twentieth century that fascist dictatorships and government-controlled corporations could overtake individual liberties if left unchecked. Only after political upheaval by the people, did Europe embarked on a market-socialist system as a stabilizing solution; a system that is becoming commonplace throughout the world.

It is critical to have an exhaustive discussion amongst the founder's roundtable (FR), so as not to repeat the same fate as other entities whose thirst for power and greed clouded their good judgment with flawed decision-making. The FR must agree to some impenetrable core values (Faith-Gratitude-Humility-Honesty-Unselfishness-Love) to ensure a high level of trust.

Without a common core belief, the notion of this endeavor being successful is unrealistic. Great leaders throughout history have come with their faults and defects. Because we are human, we are not perfect. The FR must hold true to its core values and avoids attracting unsavory characters and narcissistic personalities. The leadership across all black institutions must be revered, and the enterprise must be seen in the highest regards.

THE FOUNDATION: EMERGING AMERICAN CAPITALIST GROUP

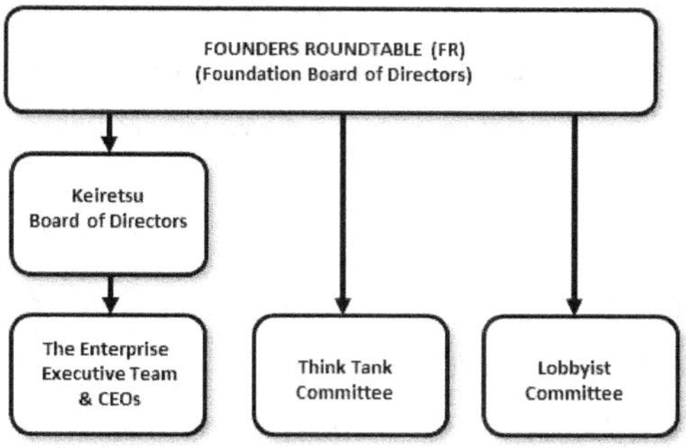

<u>Founder's Roundtable Members</u>

- Constitutional-Business Lawyers
- African American Banks
- Corporate Equity Owners
- Athletes/Entertainers
- Educators/Interfaith Council

The founder's roundtable (FR) starts out as an informal group made up of selected members to discuss and brainstorm the framework of the MEAC and adjust for the purpose of vetting and validating before engaging other key groups. Earlier attempts failed to achieve economic independence for Black people. That's why the group cannot rely on traditional relationships, like ineffective politicians, corporate America sponsorship, religious affiliations, or rebellious activism. They have all failed to deliver because in each instance there was a lack of coordination, a lack of unity and no agreed-upon outcome of the cause. More importantly, in earlier times, the Black brain trust was always exposed, and in some cases, wrongly scrutinized in a very public way. The exposure poses a severe risk to the longevity of the plan. Nobody is perfect, and that is why roles need to be well-defined, assigned, and created for public consumption. Black people need power brokers in the background, but who will eventually be recorded in the history books for doing the right things for the greater good. This strategy calls for quiet leadership to establish a reparations and reconciliation agenda that keeps the community laser focused on creating economic power, driving political decisions, and promoting a positive Black narrative. The foundation will serve as the conductor to craft the plan and write the narrative. The plan is not about radicalism or building a revolution against America. The plan is about rebranding Black people, so they are taken seriously on the world stage as competent and capable strategists who can plan and implement long-range initiatives. Black people must be willing to invest in themselves, believe in their leaders, and trust their institutions so others will invest in them too!

The FR will form the board of directors to establish official membership. The board will identify and expand African American ownership and prospective investors to participate in the enterprise based on the principles of the MEAC. A closed session will review and analyze various business and financial prospectus from various sectors for consideration. After selecting the best business targets, the ownership group will strategize a plan; map an implementation timeline depicting key milestones and action steps before establishing the board of directors and the parent company:

- Ratify Board of Director and Establish Governance By-laws
- Register as a "Corporation" (TBD)
- Select Chairman of the Board and Member's Owner Equity
- Establish Regular Meetings

The board will form the enterprise parent company and operatives of the enterprise board, as well as conduct a national search for a chief executive officer (CEO) to head the enterprise. The committee will appoint a CEO and other members of the executive team. The executive team will assume responsibility for developing the organization chart, business plan, and devise how it will leverage value innovation to disrupt targeted market. The executive team must possess experience and knowledge of key business disciplines and be prepared to mobilize people to drive the plan. The executive team will structure the organization (people, process, procedures, and policies) to ensure the enterprise achieves its profit objectives.

The enterprise will fund the think tank enabling the foundation to build synergy and connect narratives to the American people, and African Americans in particular. The think tank will utilize input data, via focused groups, including diverse laypeople, young and elderly activists, as well as other secular and religious groups to explore ways to create opportunities to invest in Black communities through training, certifications, and job placement. Another essential role of the think tank is to change how people think about the so-called "Black community". This is a more sophisticated strategy because it requires the foundation to facilitate the development of behavioral concepts to help craft new attitudes, in addition to deploying the content across various media platforms.

The enterprise will fund lobbyist committees enabling the foundation to develop language to influence legislature and monetary policies at the local, county, state, and federal levels. The primary purpose is to funnel financial support to Black entities. Also, the foundation needs people on the ground to work with industry trade groups to understand technology and trade barriers that might impact the enterprise supply change. And finally, consistent with FR core values, the lobbyist team will keep leadership aware of any sensitive social issues, and draft communications to combat negative public relations concerns.

THE EMERGING AMERICAN CAPTIALIST

Pillar 2 – Leadership is crucial because it establishes the company's ownership and governance. The enterprise may start out as a private holding company with the board of directors acting as the executive team, having oversight of all activities of the company, including its governing body to set policies and oversee management and operations.

Under the start-up status, the enterprise can raise unlimited capital under the exemption of Regulation D, while a public board must disclose information each quarter. As the enterprise reaches a certain level of maturity, the owners may elect to convert to a publicly traded holding company to raise additional capital by selling shares of ownership to the public via an Initial Public Offering (IPO). The core group of private board members make up the principal owners. Additional members may join the ownership groups through mergers and acquisitions. Members may also include private wealth managers to represent client investor groups, as well as affluent individuals. If the decision to go public materializes, about eighty-five percent of the company's shares are sold to institutional investors during the IPO, and the rest to individuals under the **Emerging American Capitalist (EAC)** umbrella. The EAC will need about $100 million in revenue before going public; a typical benchmark to give investors' confidence about the amount of time the enterprise can achieve $1 billion in revenue.

The EAC group will provide the vision and mission of the enterprise, while the CEO will focus on growing market strategies and determining profit margins from various prospectus and analysis crucial to bringing value to its members in the form of owner equity. Finally, the CEO will have the authority to hire, direct, and terminate the services of the parent company. The CEO, with the approval of the board, appoints other executive team members who are experts in the following areas:

- Entrepreneurship
- Value Innovation: Marketing and Branding
- Mergers and Acquisitions
- Portfolio Management

- Commodities and Trading
- Certified Public Accountant (CPA) – Knowledgeable of GAAP and IFRS Methods
- Information Technology and Big Data Management and Analytics
- Budget Forecasting and Enterprise Resource Planning
- Profits and Loss Management
- Talent Acquisition
- Continuous Process Improvement
- Lean Six Sigma (Manufacturing, Supply Chain and Integrated Project Development)

The executive leadership team must have the ability to develop critical market segments, products, and services with potential value. The intent is to take marginal performing operations and grow them into profit margins powerhouses.

THE EAC GROUP ORGANIZATIONAL STRUCTURE

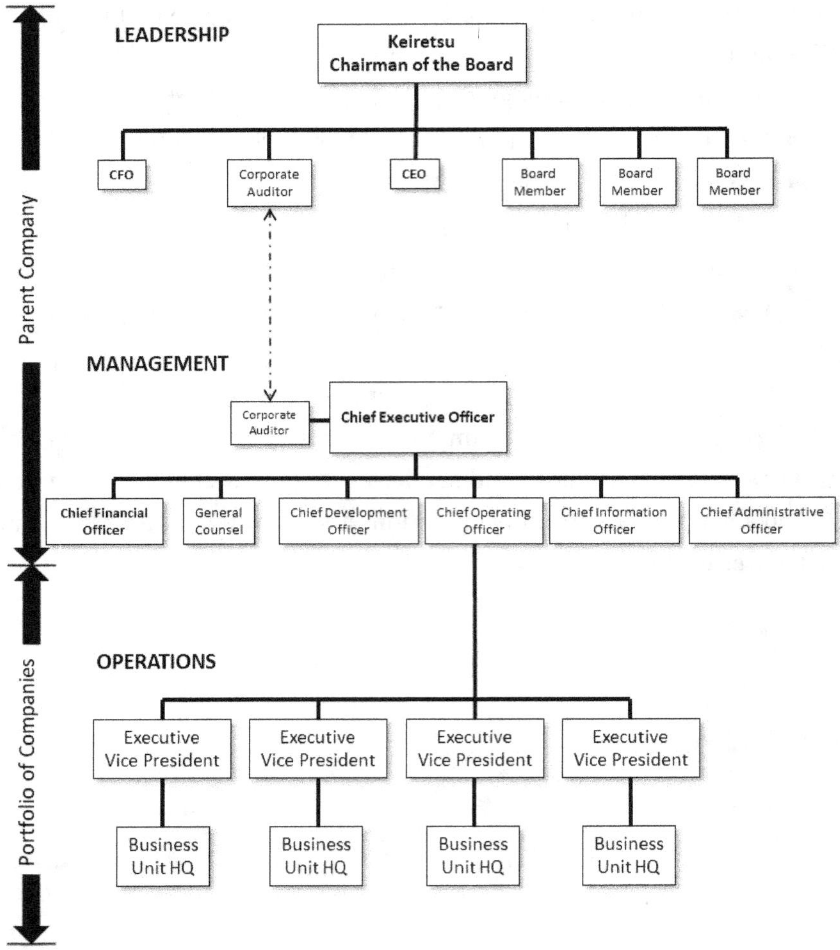

<u>Pillar 3 – Management</u> oversees four management platforms.

Resource Management

Investment Management

Risk Management

Business Management

1) *<u>Resource Management</u>* responsible for analyzing skillset requirements and developing the recruitment packages. Securing human capital capable of delivering desired business results is important. It begins with

the executive management team. The chief administrative officer will oversee this platform. The EAC must implement a process at the very start to filter out passive aggressive and combative leadership styles. Regardless of their skills and abilities, these characteristics will only be a cancer, especially if they are placed in a position of influence in the organization.

The EAC must create team environments. Building trust and creating ways of using positive conflict resolution to facilitate commitment and accountability will produce exceptional results. Even though there are different industries to manage, the ability to work as a team is imperative. Traditional silos and turf have proven ineffective and will eventually produce complacency and mediocrity. The EAC must recruit individuals who are influential leaders capable of reasoning and doing the right thing at the senior management level because people are willing to follow them. On the other hand, the company must hire good managers for operations because they do things right, and other people are eager to work with them. The Management Assessment Filter will distinguish high performers from marginal and low performers. Leadership can coach up marginal performers and place low performers in more appropriate assignments within operations. The EAC must rely on robust Enterprise Resource Planning (ERP) Systems to manage resource assets.

Enterprise Resource Management

- Talent Acquisition/Recruitment
- Onboarding/Training
- Equal Employment Opportunity
- Health Insurance/OSHA
- Payroll/Pension/Benefits
- Worker's Compensation
- Employee Assistance Program
- Separation/Retirement
- Treasury
- Accounts Payable
- Accounts Receivable
- Inventory/FIFO
- Vouchers/Petty Cash
- Banking/Credit Cards
- Contract Purchasing
- Budget Planning

2) *Investment Management* is responsible for investing in cutting-edge technologies, scientific and non-scientific start-ups to diversify beyond the corporations' common stock, treasury securities, and certificate of deposits

(CDs), including collaborative transactions and venture capitalist investments. Collaborative transactions allow the corporation to invest in new technology, start-ups, and traditional franchises. The chief financial officer (CFO) will oversee this platform. Today, clean-energy companies are funded by the arms of corporate venture-capitalist (VC) in the millions on an annual basis. The EAC will determine sectors to invest in and be willing to participate in future investments that address society's needs and expectations. While some of the opportunities presented in the next essay identify potential game changing value propositions, some may have serious policy and political ramifications, not to mention impact access to working capital. The EAC must expand its exposure to VC space. Investment banking for Black people is limited. The EAC must develop a robust portfolio of businesses to garner large pension funds, financial firms, insurance companies and university endowment investors. African American VC firms make up less than four tenth of a percent of startups in the U.S. Most startups fail to prepare a strong business plan required by major VC firms with significant capital because they failed to; a) develop a compelling investor pitch presentation, b) have a solid proof of concept of prototype and product offering, c) conduct market research and comprehensive competitive analysis, d) provide detail financial projections to demonstrate how the brand, product or service will achieve its return on investment, and e) understand the reasons why a VC may not want to fund their project.

Major VC firms must minimize risk and maximize potential blockbuster breakthroughs. If African Americans lack technical knowledge and resources, it is unlikely that they will come prepared to compete at the level required to secure VC backed funding. The mainstream investment opportunities are less volatile, especially franchises and start-ups acquired through collaborative transactions. The real benefit of investing in a well-established franchise is the low start-up cost and minimal risk. The EAC can pick and choose the best franchise and where to locate them, and high-performing franchises can double in value when sold. If you are an individual investor, the initial investment could be a barrier, and adherence to limited territory and strict marketing guidelines from parent company could impede growth. The reputation of your business could become at risk for a reason outside your control, especially if the franchise is mismanaged. If this is the investor's primary business, it could limit their exit strategy. The emergence of robotic process automation (RPA) is no longer a future concept. Today, software enables robots to execute simple to complex repetitive and routine tasks more efficiently. An infusion of artificial intelligence and workflow management will allow employees to perform other activities through accelerated critical thinking and data management applications.

3) <u>*Risk Management*</u> involves the ability to manage the enterprise during a downturn in the market, essential to sustain financial viability. The general counsel (GC), along with the corporate auditor, will oversee this platform. The EAC risk mitigation is a vital aspect of earning the trust, credibility, and confidence of stakeholders and the public. There will always be downturns in the market, typically, when the stock transition from a bull market (high value); to a bear market (hitting new low cost) where stock fails to recover to its previous high. The CFO and fund managers must be savvy to avoid temptations for bad investment bubbles like Scandinavia's banking crisis and the U.S. mortgage crisis, always being on the lookout for hubris behaviors.

The EAC should also consider slow growth of wealth funds. Most sovereign wealth funds are state-owned and invest in stock, bonds, real estate, precious metals, as well as private equity funds, and hedge funds. Collaborative financing is another new way to manage simple transactions directly between individuals without using traditional financial institutions. Collaborative deals are not a replacement for corporate banking transactions since it is crucial to managing cash flow, liquidity, and aspects of the supply chain. Every country in the world acknowledges the shift of economic power to Africa and Asia, and the EAC must invest in the region selectively due to global sanctions and political unrest around the world. Leadership on its own comes with real risk of physical harm, financial harm, loss of reputation, and accountability. Even though mitigation is possible, we must acknowledge that leadership comes with added risk. It's not a matter of competency since Black leaders are prevalent throughout corporate America.

The EAC must go through great extremes to find a strong leader who understands how to inspire people, engage management teams, and treat workers fairly, so they feel they are part of the organization. Unlike any time in history, the EAC needs people who can unify people. While it is unfair to think anything short of a saint will do, a rare person who rises above reproach with the charisma and pedigree to influence others to buy into the vision is paramount. Another risk is being able to predict uncertain times, and they will inevitably happen, so planning for uncertainty is indispensably necessary. Attacks against Black entrepreneurs are pervasive and designed to divide and conquer. Historically Black business ideas (e.g., NBA, BET, and Jet Magazine) were undermined by corporate predators, causing them to lose their fortune to larger U.S. corporation. Today, Black entrepreneurs must learn the importance of proprietary information protection and the value of patents. There are too many examples of successful Black companies going bankrupt due to bigger firms who took advantage of their inability to scale (maintain quality and profit margins). Therefore, the EAC must form conglomerates to amass an array of business models through mergers and acquisitions. These businesses must add value to the portfolio to broaden profitability and cash flow potential, minimizing the vulnerability of being dependent on limited single account revenue versus larger corporations with many products.

To determine the best firms to acquire or merge with, it helps to learn as much as possible about the targeted firm. Studies have shown three valuable approaches: 1) acquirers favor private targets in familiar industries, and then turn public and enter new business domain with higher intangible assets, 2) acquiring private targets perform better than acquiring public targets on the announcement of mergers, and 3) acquirers of private firms perform better when they acquired public firms, and conversely, a public firm performs better when they acquire a private firm. Given the constant change in the markets, it is always time for new ideas and re-imagining supply chain models. The ability to effectively communicate timely plans across the organization is crucial. We live in the age of automation, technological innovation, and market disruption. For example, Smartphones are slowly displacing multiple devices and applications that impact daily life. A person can download any app (computing application) to interact with family and friends, make purchases and schedule deliveries, as well as conduct business with team members around the world right from the palm of their hand. The EAC needs to stay abreast of consumer behavior and business trends to design desirable and robust value propositions that will resonate in the market. The EAC cannot be satisfied with following the leader with mainstream cookie-cutter franchises and brands that are void of evergreen cultural norms. If the EAC fails to identify with the long-term connectivity to people and markets will risk becoming obsolete.

4) <u>Business Management</u> integrates resources, investment, and risk management to formulate tactics to penetrate new market space. The chief development officer (CDO) and chief information officer (CIO) will oversee this platform. The "secret sauce" in the recipe for creating new market space is about having the right team who understands global markets, risk mitigation, and outside the box thinking. The premise of market disruptors starts with eliminating factors in an industry people take for granted, thus, reducing cost. At the same time, identifying factors never offered before and raising value people want or need. The EAC must develop rapid value assessments (RVA) to provide proof of concepts.

RAPID VALUE ASSESSMENT

The Rapid Value Assessement looks at businesses ranging from highly complex industries with a significant barrier to market, and low-cost investment franchises and start-ups with minimum entry barrier to market:

- Infrastructure: Urban Master Planning and Community Development, and Construction
- Product Development: Light Manufacturing (3D Printing), Supply Chain Management and Distribution, and Urban Farming
- Product and Services: Hospitality, Insurance, Health Care, Senior Care, and Consumer Goods
- Customer Experience: Remote and Virtual Experiential Lifestyle

Utilizing this business intelligence and data analytics, the management team will employ methodologies proven to help develop new products and services. The primary tool to create new market space is the Six Strategic Paths of Value Innovation developed by Blue Ocean Strategy (Chan Kim & Renee Mauborgne) and successfully used by many Fortune 500 corporations.

SIX STRATEGIC PATHS OF VALUE INNOVATION

KEY WORDS

1. Understand Rivals
2. Competitive Standing
3. Know Decision-Makers
4. Maximize Value
5. Improve Price
6. Recognize Trends

After identifying targeted businesses, the value innovation evaluation process enables the profiling of the industry and divides them up into segmentations. It is essential to determine critical decision-makers to understand industry shortcomings. This process will be helpful when mapping the value chain to look for opportunities not offered today. One of the traps business falls into is deploying costly add-ons and bundling unwanted packages in the hopes of offering complementary widgets to force customers to pay more. The EAC must not discount the importance of human unpredictability, and how people's behavior and buying habits change over time.

The six strategic path frameworks provide the basis for preparing value curves that compare the relative value of attributes between various groups, product, and service offerings.

Path one looks across industries and substitutes to understand the key threats and potential opportunities beyond the current market, asking who you are competing against. What are the alternatives to the current offering? What are the advantages or disadvantages of other options?

Path two looks across strategic groups to understand the differences in the markets and how decision-makers view trends in the market. Where are potential service lines, revenue, and profitability? Are there special strategies?

Path three looks across the chain of buyers to understand the key buyers and influencers within the market segment by examining who is typically buying the product or service. Who influences the decision? What opportunities might be provided by shifting focus to other players in the chain?

Path four looks across complementary offering by understanding augmenting product and services. What is typically sold as part of the offering? Who influences the decision? What opportunities might be considered to enhance the buying experience?

Path five looks across the functional and emotional appeal through six utility levers. Functional levers include customer productivity, simplicity, and convenience, while emotional levers include Lowering risk, fun and image, as well as environmental friendliness.

Path six looks across time and trends to understand changes that occurred in buying habits, and behaviors. Who is buying what, when and where and how? What influential media is playing a role? What challenges will be facing the segment?

VALUE CURVES

The value curves allow the comparison of any strategic path against a set of attributes to create, refine and analyze value chain. Attributes composed of ease of use, cost, time, and barriers to market entry. The value curve allows triangulation of distribution channel, customize market and optimize business value.

Pillar 4 – Operations is where the rubber meets the road. The Chief Operating Officer (COO) will oversee operations. Beyond having smart people (leadership) at the helm who are financially astute and organized, most well-managed businesses understand profitability levers, are always measuring key performance indicators (KPI), also referred to (Keep People Interested) to determine its success or failure. If the business unit can reduce process variation and wasteful steps across all its business units and supply chain, it can master the kind of agility to drive growth during good times and maintain cash flow during the lean times. Continuous improvement begins with leadership who utilizes quantifiable information and analysis to develop strategic planning capable of managing quality systems and principles will produce the best results.

The EAC doesn't have to reinvent the wheel; continuous improvement methodologies already exist but will require strong and intelligent leaders who can manage and execute the following steps. First, identify the kind of output or desired results envision for the targeted business unit. Next, identify the customers who buy the goods and services and determine their requirements. Then, translate those customer requirements into specifications and develop processes, and measurements to capture KPIs associated with customer needs. The EAC must have the ability to identify problems and prioritize improvement opportunities in real-time. The EAC must adopt ways to continuously improve work processes, update procedures, adjust policies, and train people to create an environment of high performing teams. The EAC must be committed to excellence through its people. The goal is to provide the best value to customers, work environment for employees and profits to shareholders. Regardless of the product or service type, every business unit has performance measures, and represents the most significant opportunity for any business venture. The objective is to equip the unit vice presidents and managers with the tools to execute the plan. The practices of quality assurance, quality control, and quality business systems and methodologies like Lean Six Sigma and ISO-Certification are commonplace across most industries today. Only the best organizations adopt these methodologies as part of their culture. Developing ways to maintain high standards requires the ability to repeat the customer experience repeatedly; otherwise, brand loyalty will diminish rapidly.

CONTINUOUS PROCESS IMPROVEMENT (CPI)

For every existing business, merger, acquisition, or start-up of the enterprise, the EAC must sort and organize the business unit by documenting processes. From sales and marketing, customer databases, product and services profile to supply chain and distribution channels, and invoicing for account receivables. Conducting a comprehensive analysis will help better understand customer requirements and potential opportunities. The DuPont Continuous Process Improvement (CPI) methodology is a proven approach to achieve a world-class organization:

QUESTIONS *ANSWERS*

1. What is our product or service output? *A statement to describe output*
2. What do our customers require? *A single list of customer requirements*
3. How can we ensure our outputs meet customer requirements? *Customer consensus*
4. How do we generate our output? *Create a flow diagram order-to-cash work process*
5. What should we measure? *Customer consensus – list "vital few" measurements*
6. What improvements should we make? *Internal Consensus as to what to improve first*
7. What is the best way to implement the improvements? *Implemented improvements*
8. How effective are the improvements? *Verify improvement effectiveness*
9. How can we sustain the improvements? *Generate evidence of sustained improvements*

By setting things in order and establishing measurement systems used to track outputs. CPI tools (e.g., Criteria Rating Form, "As-Is" Workflow Process Maps, and Cause & Effect Diagrams) can provide an overview of performance measurement systems and ensure what to measure and how to perform measures that reflects actual outputs.

CAUSE & EFFECT DIAGRAM (aka FISHBONE DIAGRAM)

To ensure accuracy of procedures, processes, and production outputs, additional CPI tools (e.g., "To-Be" Workflow Process Maps, Multi-voting Techniques, Pareto Diagrams, and other statistical methodologies) are used to analyze variables targeted to specific areas needing improvement. This will expose skill-gaps and technology deficiencies as it relates to methods, materials, management, and mitigation of potential risk.

WORKFLOW PROCESS MAP

To ensure the organization achieved stabilization of operations. CPI tools (e.g., run charts, Gantt charts, histograms and scatter plots) will help to monitor and standardize processes, procedures, products, and people. This is an opportunity to leverage best practices observed through benchmarking examination from other businesses in the portfolio.

RUN CHART

To continuously improve quality and level of services, (e.g., automated run charts, control charts, check sheets, and customer interviews), the EAC must maintain standard operating procedures, maintain calibration limits, and conduct daily quality assurance statistics and reporting. These data validate and ensure control of standards and specifications.

Finally, the Plan, Do, Check, and Act (PDCA) Cycle provides a constant review of new business processes, products, and services, especially defining repetitive work processes, planning data collection, and analysis to verify problems, and root causes or to implement change.

It is easy to read through an operations quality assurance manual to understand how the CPI works, but it is very challenging to implement. To change people, especially people accustomed to performing their jobs in a certain way, is difficult. In a merger and acquisition situation, eliminating redundant laborers, wasteful work processes and inefficient equipment and technology can be daunting. Regardless of the type of business, product, or service, the EAC must find ways to optimize all aspects of managing the enterprise, including all aspects related to customer experience.

CUSTOMER EXPERIENCE

The EAC must create a new paradigm when it comes to human interaction and the ability to get paid for cultivating relationships, catering to human senses, and providing purpose through an experiential lifestyle to counteract the impersonal low-cost e-commerce transactional exchange deployed today. With the large segments of the population emerging towards remote working will have a profound impact on traditional work-life balance and interpersonal relationships.

The EAC has an opportunity to reinvent retail, commercial and residential spaces, integrating a mass-production lifestyle for the common family like Ford Motor Company did in making an automobile accessible to everyone. The EAC must reinvent Customer Experience as a Service (CEaaS); from hospitality to healthcare, CEaaS will eventually supersede traditional customer service ideas, as people begin to reimagine its need to connect with other humans across the globe. The evolution of virtual reality will challenge the construct of social gatherings, even traditional gladiator sports could be threatened. How we live will shape how our communities are designed and equipped to sustain life. The early adopters and pioneers who can create these new markets to solve the needs of society will succeed.

Conventional wisdom defines customer service as the support you offer your customers from the beginning to the end of the value chain process, helping them in a functional and enjoyable manner. CEaaS is about delivering customer service on a deeper experiential level to ensure you retain customers for life. It means everyone from the top leaders to the front line staff must embody customer needs ahead of everything else.

If everyone in the organization follows the best practice of valuing a customer's time, will leave an impression that customers will alway remember. And it will go a long way if employees are well-trained and knowledgeable about the products and services being offered, and resourceful when it comes to meeting and exceeding the customer's needs.

The world is getting smaller and entering into a new frontier as we merge technology and human interaction, and the thought of limiting one's brands, products and services to "me-too" offering is not sustainable. African Americans are people with high expectations but must come to terms with their own businesses and how they present them, not only to other people, but especially the Black people. African American reparations will take more than demanding equality and social justice. It will require vision, leadership, and determination beyond the physical expression to capture the imagination, hearts, and minds of the American people.

The enterprise must harness its collective assets in a way that allows the EAC to strengthen its balance sheet and investment worthiness which will take shape in the forms of new brands, products, and services. The EAC must take business opportunities to a new level. The next essay goes beyond the exploration of existing and new sectors by applying value innovation in a way that carves out new market space not available today.

The EAC sets out to demonstrate the most compelling markets that will drive synergy amongst all Americans, but more importantly, provides a vehicle to enable the inclusion of African Americans in a meaningful way. Innovation is where the rubber meets the road. Creating new spaces is only the beginning. Once you capture the new market, you must fight to keep it relevant! Great inventions like the Swiss watch were supplanted by LED watches. AOL My Space was replaced by Facebook. And there is no reason why the CEaaS cannot overtake tech giants like Amazon and Google by understanding how we connect to the needs of human beings, now and in the future.

By ensuring the needs of your customers are met and the values of your business model adheres to the ideas of your customers will earn their trust and maintain customer loyalty. There is a good reason why certain companies are successful, and others go out of business. There is a reason why certain communities stand out over others. Successful people understand the importance of continuous improvement and never resting on their laurels.

The CEaaS concept is about reimagining everything! Lifestyles in the future are about a journey and not a destination; redefining the ways we live is about living for a purpose. With the weakening of organized religion around the world, being of service to others has dramatically diminished as the secular population become more disenfranchised by materialism and greed. The power of service to human beings is a lost art. Once restored, African Americans cannot be seduced by the pitfalls of short-sightedness. The foundation and the enterprises must formulate an EAC marketplace that will create a new transformative way to advance society for all.

THE MARKETS

Ideas are great, but you must have a long-range plan and the financial means to carry them out. We have all heard someone talk about a big idea. In some cases, it may have been a good idea, and even a profitable one. Don't be mistaken, good ideas are even better when they are accompanied by a clear vision and backed by real money.

A major challenge facing human beings is the ever-growing population on earth with the human population approaching 7.8 billion people. It is unwise for people to believe we can continue to populate the earth indefinitely without consequences. I don't know if climate change will destroy the earth, but I can say that a natural or man-made catastrophic event, e.g., a meteor or nuclear war could make the world uninhabitable for human life.

Over the course of many civilizations, humans observed nature and adapted to the various environmental conditions, thus, harvesting the scarcity of natural resources and finding innovative ways to enhance human comfort and survival. It is inevitable human beings will always encounter vicissitudes of life, and it has been the market that continues to play a critical role in addressing the problems facing world issues.

African Americans have a unique opportunity to become unified and overcome the issue that plagued its people since the founding of America. One way to start the process is to create an economy of scale to enable Black people to advance the country, something inconceivable in the past.

THE MARKETS

- **PREFACE**
- **INTRODUCTION**
- **VALUE INNOVATION**
- **THE BRANDS, PRODUCTS, AND SERVICES**

PREFACE

This white paper details innovation of new and existing market segments. The reader may recall from my previous paper, I asserted that there are no industries out of bound to value innovation. Regardless of revamping a mature business or re-imaging a new start-up migrating into uncharted territory. Ingenuity and adequate capital are essential to enable entrepreneurs to develop proof of concepts before disrupting the market. The global economy is estimated at around $80 trillion. The United States, China followed by Japan round out the top economies in the world. It is well documented that the U.S. economy is estimated at $12 to $18 trillion. The government's stimulus package to support the economy impacted by the coronavirus pandemic (COVID-19) is expected to produce an artificial recession. The initial government bailout (aka, CARES Act) of $4 trillion went to large corporations, including airlines and airports. For companies, both medium to small had to weather the storm, as the recovery is expected to be slow, according to some experts. Subsequent government stimulus programs were implemented to support small businesses, e.g., the Payroll Protection Plan (PPP). During the 2008 Great Recession, large corporations used government bailouts to buyback corporate stock. Many executives cashed in dividends while allocating very little to future corporate rainy-day funds, which explained why economist watchdogs were so perplexed to learn that the COVID-19 bailout was so critical to help these same large corporations sustain their balance sheet. As a result, Congress inserted legislation to prevent large corporations from using taxpayer backed stimulus funds for stock buybacks. While the world economies experienced an unprecedented shutdown, it will inevitably rebound. New business models will emerge and supplant outdated industries and obsoleted goods and services with newer and more relevant products. The early innovators of the United States created generational wealth for their families, and many are still around today. Dating back to the American Revolution, E. I. du Pont de Nemours supplied ammunition to the U.S. military through many American conflicts up to War World II. Other giant industrialists built great wealth and political power like Cornelius Vanderbilt (1794-1877), who became a railroad tycoon. John D. Rockefeller (1839-1937) became the richest man in history as an Oil Magnate. During the lifetime of Andrew Carnegie (1837-1919) became a steel baron and philanthropist, and J.P. Morgan became a financier and champion of the Electric Light. And where would the world be without the mobility innovation of Henry Ford (1863-1947)? Mr. Ford became the captain of industry by revolutionizing the automobile manufacturing process. Imagine the wealth if your families made an impact on society. Since the launch of Facebook there are claims that it will create 1,000 millionaires. New entrepreneurs like Google and Amazon emerged as e-Commerce technology giants, producing unlimited and untapped potential consumer value. As with the early innovators mentioned above, the growth of technology giants like Facebook, Google and Amazon come with a double-edge sword, as nearly half of Americans believe the U.S. government should impose antitrust violations against these firms. This is not unprecedented in American history, as similar sentiments surfaced in the country when Standard Oil and AT&T once dominated the oil and communications market and had to be broken up because they became a monopoly, preventing competition.

The thought here is for the Emerging American Capitalist (EAC) to think about how it will drive social changes through market innovation. While Black people are preoccupied with social injustices, the innovators of tomorrow are thinking about those things unspoken and not publicized. The recent space launch of Space-X used to transport cargo to the International Space Station (ISS) is an example of conquering new frontiers, as outer space could provide new markets and enable future generations the ability to enjoy commercial space travel. Scientists are being funded by wealthy aristocrats to conduct research to learn how humans can survive in the unpredictability of outer space. The U.S., Europe, Russia, Japan, and Canada have been operating the ISS for more than 22 years at costs north of $150 billion. Black people cannot afford to languish amid these emerging new markets. If there is a prolong failure to act, Black people around the world will continue to fall behind lessening any chances of leveling the playing field. The U.S. has 607 billionaires and only six of them are Black. How did these Black billionaires achieve their fortune? Unlike the DuPont's, Vanderbilts,

Rockefeller's, Carnegie's, Morgan's and Ford's, there are no Black industrialists or financiers amongst them. Only European billionaires have exclusive control over industrialization and capital apparatuses to perpetuate institutional wealth for their descendants well into the next millennial. Black wealth is not a sustainable arrangement, as it stands, and will only maintain a widen wealth gap, create social inequality, and propagate racial resentment for future generations. African Americans need a succession plan that will lead to real social change and upward mobility for its people. There is a lot of talk about how the minorities can take advantage of government sponsored financial mechanism like the Economic Opportunity Zones (EOZ), the Economic Development District (EDD), and the Public Private Partnerships (PPP) to boost capital and expand their investment capabilities, but it's not enough. Only though asset consolidation, mergers and acquisition of existing enterprises and land ownership can African Americans create the type of power needed to take control of its own destiny. I spent most of my career measuring corporate performance, analyzing, and implementing solutions to add value to products and improve processes to generate revenue growth and profitability. I have witnessed the characteristics of great companies first-hand. These companies started out with charismatic and imaginative leaders with a vision and access to capital to drive vertical and horizontal growth of their company. Also, they had the ability and capacity to reinvent the company over many generations. If large companies fail to change with time, it is not uncommon for new products to come along and disrupt an entire industry to the point of eliminating them from the market. An early example is the Japanese automakers who were known for producing poor quality cars until quality guru, William Deming (a former Ford Motor Company engineer), introduced them to Total Quality Management (TCM). They used the Voice of the Customer (VOC) and translated the data into Critical to Quality (CTQ) milestones and measurable deliverables to change the automotive industry we know today. To go a step further, the Japanese automakers enhanced its global quality image by selling defective products within their domestic markets and exporting only the best products abroad to change the rest of the world's perception about the quality of their cars. The Korean automakers followed the same model, making the Japanese and Korean automakers amongst the top selling vehicles in the world, and at one point outperforming General Motors, Ford Motor Company, and Daimler-Chrysler.

Today, new entrants are transforming the mobility industry, yet again, as the internet of things, combining software, autonomous (self-driving) capability and electrification is changing the way we think about transportation. All traditional manufacturers in this space must change or risk becoming obsolete. With the rise of new conglomerates like the Carlyle Group, founded in 1987, demonstrates the power of consolidated private equity, asset management and financial services.

After decades of failed set-asides sponsored government schemes designed to appease the African American political class, it has become self-evident that Black people cannot rely on the United States government alone. The U.S. Government Small Business Administration (SBA) and other state and local government procurement programs provide little value in the long run. These initiatives will never lead to real wealth due in part to state and local municipalities who administer ordinances. The projects are usually small in nature and maintain paltry inclusion language. They impose barriers like minimum qualifications that disproportionately disqualify Black-owned enterprises as non-responsive and non-responsible, thus restricting their participation, and allows bureaucrats to decide the winners and losers. The Emerging American Capitalist (EAC) must shift the business approach of using Black people to secure joint-venture contracts where retired popular athletes and other self-serving individuals act as the front-person for so-called minority-owned businesses and do little to support their own people. African Americans must be in the position to hire its own people and ensure they share in the benefits of real business ownership; a requirement necessary to produce institutional wealth and political influence to triumph the post-slavery mindset. The EAC has three major challenges to overcome; 1) changing the perception of the corrupt Black politicians or post-athlete/hip-hop celebrity gets-rich persona, 2) persuade wealthy Black people to consolidate and leverage its capital to acquire and innovate various industries to create transformative high-quality products and brands with exceptional customer service, and 3) foster a new reality of professionalism and competence when you think about African American led businesses. It's unfortunate that some successful leaders and power brokers on the African continent, including some African American leaders in the U.S. who rose to national prominence, have become seduced into selling out and turning their backs on their own people. It wasn't always that way. As a child, I recalled being taught not to forget where you came from. We used to believe in helping our people get ahead. It's wonderful to accomplish the goal of getting rich, but now what? The concept of the leisure society taught in sociology during the 1960s – 1970s is a myth concocted in the 19th century. The trend of people working less hours would continue indefinitely is a misnomer. Instead, entrepreneurs must find new ways to gainfully employ the masses in a real productive way. People are thinkers, inventors, and creators always seeking to advance its species in a way that continuously adapts to whatever environment that impacts their survival. How do we put our people to work?

INTRODUCTION

The need for human interaction will always adjust and normalize to accommodate new forms of transactions and commerce. Despite the constant shift in business practices, successful entrepreneurs must discover new breakthrough strategies to navigate the labyrinth of high-tech cyber security and automation, while still maintaining ways to nurture human connections. The Emerging American Capitalist (EAC) will need to rethink the labor landscape and re-imagine the functionality of future factories, supply chain, and channels to markets. Value innovation is an essential component that overlays the spectrum of goods and services, and more importantly, determines how products are produced and delivered across the region, around the world, and into outer space. To review, there are four dominant types of economies: 1) Traditional, 2) Command, 3) Market, and 4) Mixed. The traditional economy (e.g., the Jarawa tribe of the Andaman Islands) is a monopoly, where a high order of the tribe dictates decisions regarding the economy. The Command economy (e.g., China, North Korea, and Cuba) is more advanced than the traditional economy; such that, the economic system is controlled by a single centralize power. The market economy (e.g., the United States of America) is driven by supply and demand of goods and services. The mixed economy (e.g., western European states), relies on a mix of markets and command economic characteristics. Some economies rely on predominant commodities that are highly volatile and can disproportionally affect a country's Gross Domestic Products (GDP) more than any other commodity. For example, Crude Oil in the Middle East changed the lives of people living in the countries like Saudi Arabia, Iran, Iraq, and Kuwait, resulting in unrivaled wealth, political influence and social stability that kept their economy moving in a positive direction. However, volatility in the price of a barrel of oil can cause severe consequences to their domestic economy and prone to investors trading oil prices against the U.S. currency. Another example is the reliance on a military economy, which caused the collapse of the former Union of Soviet Socialist Republics (USSR) due to an international arms race competition with the West. Today, western market economies like the United States still allocates twenty-nine percent of its $3.79 trillion annual budget for discretionary spending, of which, fifty percent goes towards its military complex to ensure its ability to mobilize its economy for wartime production if needed. In simple terms, successful markets come down to supply & demand for certain goods and services, where prices and quantities are inversely related. If prices decrease, the quantity demanded increases. If income increases with the change in price, the demand curve will shift with an even greater quantity demanded. Innovation is about bringing these goods and services to the market with the greatest value and least cost to deliver. If there is stability across the planet, markets will thrive. Every product, brand, and service from every sector of the economy, including banking, energy, engineering infrastructure, business development, and community development, to skilled trades, education and space exploration is subjective to value innovation. Nothing is out of bounds and is only limited by your imagination. Prior to the pandemic, the U.S. economy was building momentum. Because of the cyclical nature of the market economy, many Black proprietors did not survive, as they lacked the necessary capital to sustain operations. Black people must stop giving away their ideas for others to capitalize. They have always been innovative throughout American history, from technical and scientific inventions to art, music, and entertainment. Take the National Basketball Association (NBA) for example. Black players: pre-dating the Harlem globetrotters had already mastered the high-flying streetball playing style, complete with food and a half-time carnival atmosphere.

The American Basketball Association (ABA) and NBA repackaged professional basketball during the Julius "Dr. J" Erving era and then transformed the game entirely during the Ervin "Magic" Johnson era, producing billions of dollars for white team owners. The NBA produced many rich Black players, but most lost their riches soon after leaving the game. A few notables like Michael Jordan became a billionaire. Early musicians and entertainers were exploited too; having their songs and dance moves rewritten and choreograph for white musicians to perform for their audiences. Historical Black powerhouses like Madam CJ Walker beauty products, and Johnson Publications, Insurance, health, and beauty products no longer exist. What happened to them? Black people lost billions in generational wealth because their interest was not protected due to no succession plan. Regardless of whether their ideas were registered in the US patent office, African Americans did not have sustaining power to endure the longevity of their inventions, products, and services. And even on the rare occasion when they could be a formidable competitor, were eventually seduced in selling out to a well-financed European company. There is security in numbers as seen across the various sectors. There are lots of opportunities for Black people to break into new markets in a big way, but they must work together. The aerospace industry made huge strives after the coronavirus outbreak with the help of the government bailout. The rebound took less than two years. According to experts, the impact will be short-lived for manufacturing too. While one door closes, another one opens, and this might be the case, as drones are likely to emerge for urban passenger travel and last mile package deliveries. The space sector is also expected to continue its rapid growth and provide new opportunities in satellite communications. Even solar energy farms are not that far away from reality. Food production remains essential for human life. Everything from livestock, planting crops to servicing machinery and equipment must be an ongoing process in the farming supply chain. The COVID-19 crisis highlighted the lack of healthy food choices in certain segments of the populations of the country, only emphasizes the need to diversify food source options. Bringing food sources closer to the masses will be critical to avoid reliance on distanced crops and immigrant labor disputes. It is only a matter of time before we make the switch to renewable energy on a massive scale to leverage energy sources like wind, solar and biofuel coupled with battery storage technology, including safer nuclear energy plants. Climate change will force our hands to significantly reduce carbon gas emission or face serious health risk to world populations. Advancement in mobility and Mobility as Service (MaaS) will reimagine people's movement through space and time in an environmentally friendly way. Imagine the implications of applying for home improvement loans and new home mortgages representing new opportunities for the EAC. Domestic manufacturing of medicine and personal protective equipment (PPE) will find a permanent place in the U.S.

from sourcing, warehousing, and distributing just as the Tool and Die of specialty metals and fabrication industry saw an increase just a few decades ago. The pandemic revealed serious vulnerabilities in the country when it became apparent hospital systems could not acquire enough ventilators for patients or face masks and other PPE to protect healthcare workers. On another front, remote doctor visits and exams will emerge to make diagnoses, provide treatment, and prescribe medication, via virtual medical practices. Multi-modal logistics shippers saw a jump in revenue during the pandemic, as air cargo carriers across the board stepped up operations to meet demand. Commercial logistic firms like FedEx, United Postal Service and US Postal Service had to adjust to accommodate the movement of important artifacts, industrial parts, and medicines.

The pandemic necessitated the need for the logistics and distribution industry to move towards automation and robotics to pick and process customer orders. The resurgence of domestic manufacturing will increase storage capacity requiring more warehouse space. Domestic manufacturing will increase with more reliance on agile 3D printing for both home and traditional office workstations. There is $15 billion of pent-up global demand for new manufacturing of products and an adaptability of new mobility and supply chain is expected to boost U.S. production. The real estate market is expected to recover slowly, with industrial properties being the first to see growth. Once employment rebounds, first-time home buyers will infuse residential (single-family homes and condominiums) demand. The commercial, retail and office segment will be last out the gate, as there is still too much inventory that came out of the earlier speculative construction boom. Because of social distancing, professional sports teams lost billions in revenue, not to mention the millions of fans who missed out on an entire season of communal pass-time at various stadiums, ball parks and arenas around the country. Many college student athletes lost a full year of in-class collaboration and competing in NCAA activities. Major airlines, cruises, destination vacation resorts, and retail outlets of all stripes were hit hardest during the pandemic, especially small businesses like restaurants, fitness centers, salons, massage parlors, tattoo shops and other face-to-face services struggled to survive. Similarly, night clubs, concert goers and places of worship suffered too. In the avid of instant COVID-19 testing, digital screening, and the development of effective vaccines that detect and slow down infections will allow the world to turn the page and move onto the next chapter. What's the problem with large banks helping small Black businesses and start-ups recover? One major criticism is it keeps them poor and dependent. For example, the financial model of micro-loans helped Black woman start-up new low-tech businesses with minimal barriers to entry, but the loans usually come with high-interest rates they may never overcome. While programs like these are needed and appropriate, it's not the scale for African American reparations. These relationships between Black entrepreneurs and large financial institutions are extremely important but must be aligned for succession in a deliberate way – one that makes small companies whole over time rather than leaving outcomes to chance. It is a false premise to expect inclusion to mean people who are under-represented. It is nothing more than a "woke" talking point and disingenuous to believe working poor can achieve economic equity through predatory loans and government sponsored programs without a way to grow in the long run. Entrepreneurs are constantly looking for ways to advance new markets, from supply chain to the transportation of people, goods, and services. And technology (e.g., internet of things, biometrics, and artificial intelligence) will be at the core to address the ever-changing needs of consumers (e.g., Food/Shelter/Security, Love/Belonging, Self-Esteem, and Self-Actualization). How will it get done? Who is going to be the next generation of innovators and future market disrupters? What are the next economic engines to ignite prosperity for America? The enterprise discussed the vision, mission, core values, organizational structure and managerial expertise required to lead, manage, and execute the objectives and deliver measurable results. Regardless of the market segment, the EAC must be able to find new space and create value that other companies and individual consumers would be willing to spend their money. To provoke your thinking, a series of Technology, Entertainment, Design (TED) talk-like vignettes will be used to illustrate potential markets and value innovation opportunities.

VALUE INNOVATION

Let's recap value innovation through real-life examples. When assessing the value of an idea, the business type could range from highly complex industries with significant barriers to low-cost franchises and start-ups with minimum entry barrier to market. The six strategic path frameworks provide the basis for preparing value curves that compare the relative value of attributes between various groups, product, and service offerings.

Path one looks across industries and substitutes to understand the key threats and potential opportunities beyond the current market, asking who you are competing against. What are the alternatives to the current offering? What are the advantages or disadvantages of other options?

Path two looks across strategic groups to understand the differences in the markets and how decision-makers view trends in the market. Where are potential service lines, revenue, and profitability? Are there special strategies?

Path three looks across the chain of buyers to understand the key buyers and influencers within the market segment by examining who is typically buying the product or service. Who influences the decision? What opportunities might be provided by shifting focus to other players in the chain?

Path four looks across complementary offering by understanding how to augment products and services. What is typically sold as part of the offering? Who influences the decision? What opportunities might be considered to enhance the buying experience?

Path five looks across the functional and emotional appeal through six utility levers. Functional levers include customer productivity, simplicity, and convenience, while emotional levers include Lowering risk, fun and image, as well as environmental friendliness.

Path six looks across time and trends to understand changes that occurred in buying habits, and behaviors. Who is buying what, when where and how? What influential media is playing a role? What challenges will be facing the segment?

By utilizing rapid value assessment, the entrepreneur can test its hypothesis in the real world to determine the sweet spot for new opportunities.

In all cases, reducing cost and increasing value will produce the desired outcome. Firms that simply bundle add-ons to increase their revenue without demonstrating tangible value will not be successful creating sustainable new market space.

BOOKKEEPING: MARKET DISRUPTER BUSINESS CASE #1

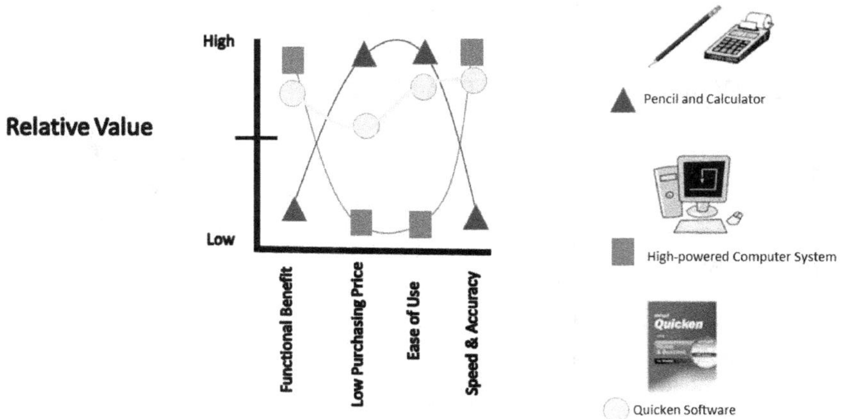

One of the simplest examples to illustrate the power of value curves is to show how Intuit, Inc., and later purchased by H.I.G. Capital, positioned their new product aimed at a wide cross-section of user groups. Quicken software compared its product to the pencil-calculator combination and high-powered computer systems. By evaluating the software against several attributes obtained through the rapid value assessment process revealed a specific curve profile. The purpose of the curve is to graphically show cost reduction, while raising value. In this case, the pencil and calculator had the lowest functional capability than the high-powered computer system and Quicken software. On the other hand, the pencil and calculator had the lowest price compared to computers and software. The pencil and calculator are easy to use, without hours of expensive training. However, quicken software, like the high-powered computer system provided speed and accuracy whereas the pencil and calculator are prone to human error.

Quicken software found the sweet spot by eliminating unnecessary features embedded in the high-powered computer system, while raising the value over the pencil-calculator by offering user-friendly functional software that was fast and accurate at a reasonable price acceptable to customers. Quicken was able to open a whole new market of do-it-yourselfers for small business that allowed them to manage their payroll and prepare taxes accurately and timely. Now, small companies could run leaner by reducing hours of tabulating and computing figures, streamlining staff, and eliminating the need to outsource professional services.

MOBILITY: MARKET DISRUPTER BUSINESS CASE #2

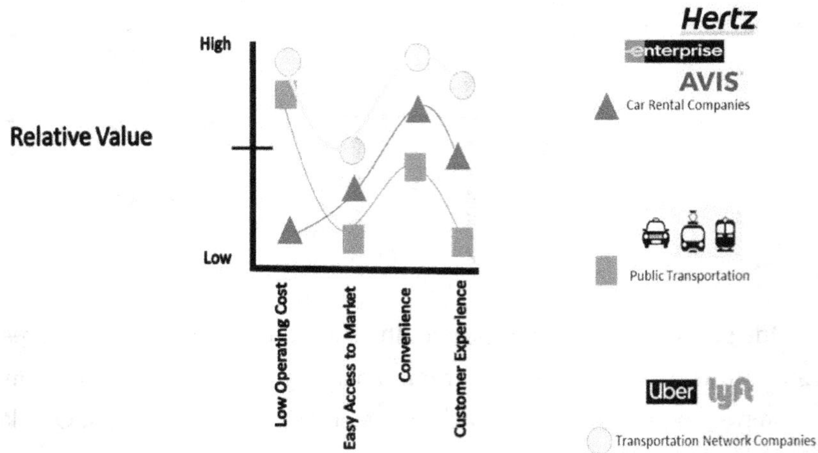

Another simple example to illustrate the power of value curves is to share how Transportation Network Companies (TNC), e.g., Uber and Lyft positioned their new offering aimed at densely populated urban areas. Uber and Lyft compared their ridesharing concept to car rental companies and public transportation, including taxi cabs. Again, the evaluation used several attributes obtained through the rapid value assessment process to produce a curve profile. In this case, the TNCs demonstrated the lowest operating cost, whereas car rental companies, limo-taxi services, and mass-transit have huge maintenance and labor costs. TNCs are easy and convenient since the user initiates the schedule on their terms, while other mobility options are priced competitively or even less than the TNC, the customer experience of mass-transit is lacking, and limo-taxi services requires long wait times. Car rental companies are tied to major airport systems and offer higher customer experience but are not fully integrated into communities where users begin their journey.

TNCs found the sweet spot by eliminating the unnecessary high-cost of operation barriers associated with car rental companies and limo-taxicab services (fleet maintenance, maintaining brick and mortar facility, as well as staffing agents-dispatchers), while raising the value over mass-transit by providing reliable services with enhanced customer experience. TNCs were able to open a whole new market space that allowed individual car owners to earn extra money using their personal vehicle like a taxi. The emergence of Uber and Lyft served as a market disrupter to these other modes of transportation. Even if new market space is created, the product lifecycles must be taken into consideration, as competitors and new technology are constantly at opposing ends of the spectrum seeking to protect established market shares.

THE BRANDS, PRODUCTS, AND SERVICES

The rise in big sector innovations; from space travel to combating climate change' impact on the environment is at an all-time high. These innovations are creating new commercial products, overcoming many challenges that prevented the implementation of solutions once thought only in science fiction movies. The U.S. passage of the congressional Bipartisan Infrastructure Law (BIL) signaled the country's commitment towards an emergence of the innovation age. There is much skepticism about the law's framework, from the lack of diversity and inclusion to the considerable uncertainty about the cost-benefit of renewable energy deployment versus consumer demand for reliable fossil fuel, especially amid the geo-political crisis in Europe and the Ukrainian conflict with Russia. Business leaders, engineers, and landscape architects amongst other planning professionals and entrepreneurs have an important role to help shape public policies to ensure society can sustain urban communities by reducing reliance on crude oil, eliminating congestion and pollution through mass transit and electric autonomous mobility, while at the same time improving public safety, education, and wellness. Throughout history, entrepreneurs are people who capitalized on opportunities and made things happen rather than waiting around for something to happen – regardless of their intentions; good or bad. Let's leave no doubt, a lack of education and limited access to capital will not produce future wealth for Black people. While some will argue many successful entrepreneurs were college dropouts, citing the likes of Oprah Winfrey, Steve Jobs, and Mark Zuckerberg. Here are some facts, Oprah, albeit, suffered great personal harm as a child, attended Milwaukee's Lincoln High School Upward Bound program before transferring to the affluent suburban Nicolet High School where she received a quality education. Steve Jobs was a B and C student, but lived in Paulo Alto' Silicon Valley, where lived next to an engineer who worked for Hewlett-Packard (HP). His neighbor had an electronic workshop in his garage where Steve spent a lot of his time. He later enrolled in the HP Explorers Club where he saw engineers demonstrate new products personally. Mark Zuckerberg attended the elite Phillips Exeter

Academy (high school), where he won prizes in mathematics, astronomy, physics, and classical studies. In these high-profile cases, a formal college degree was not necessary because they received a solid foundation early in life. In summary, they were prepared. All it took was for the opportunity to knock and they seized the moment and went after their goals without fear of failure.

When it comes to serving future customers, the EAC must become obsessed with customer engagement and experiential offerings that go beyond popular celebrity private labeled brands. With the entrenchment of online commerce, one might think the days are gone when people are excited about physical senses of smelling touching, and hearing the market experience, but without the human touch, some people come away feeling disappointed and unfulfilled. Black-owned companies must overcome the perception of lacking professionalism, not being on time, and being inattentive, disengaged, and untrustworthy, especially amongst their own people. African Americans must stop chasing from behind and leap over the competition just as they performed in sports and entertainment. What can't be ignored when it comes to the new era of Black thinkers? Is the promotion of Black collaboration and leveraging its collective knowledge to achieve wealth and political power, and only then, will African Americans win support beyond the racial divide. While the BIL could be a great moment for all Americans, for African Americans, it could serve as a catalyst for reparations and reconciliation. If African Americans were granted a portion of the BIL, the EAC could strategically invest money and consolidate its own technical expertise to compete for large-scale infrastructure contracts. At the end of day, innovation comes down to the means, abilities, and qualifications to differentiate from the competition. We will examine various types of markets the EAC must consider as part of its physical and human infrastructure plan: (nationalize banking system, early child development & higher education, land ownership & development, engineering, technology & skilled trades, religion, politics & governance, and work-life & leisure) and see how the value chain cycles are tied to specific inputs and desired outcomes. The market analysis examines the participants, revenue streams, and other demographics as it pertains to the dominant players amongst the targeted markets. We will examine how money is made, via, order to cash along the value chain, e.g., retail, and commercial operations, supply chain of raw material and distribution delivery systems, and channels to market. We will examine technical challenges, e.g., research & development, proprietary knowledge, and expertise requirements which typically translate into market barriers such as capital, regulatory, and certification requirements. At the end of each industry type, we will introduce a value proposition of potential unclaimed white space in the market.

BANKING & FINANCIAL INDUSTRY

For the EAC to be successful, it must amass enough capital at an accelerated rate to create African American wealth. Without a reparations provision, it will never happen. A renowned British historian, Niall Ferguson, published the Ascent of Money that examined the origin of money dating back centuries. He described the financial history of the world dating back to ancient times leading to the development of insurance to the formation of banking systems and then the stock market. It was during the Constantine Christians period where the Jewish Publicans would provide the genesis of loans. At that time, Christian's frown upon the practice of lending money in exchange of future earnings. Over the centuries that followed, the practice gave way to the Rothschild, the richest family in the history of the world, controlling nearly a quarter of the world's wealth today. Wealth was controlled through minted coin currency, tracing back to Silver, Gold and later backed by commodities like cotton and coal. Today, the U.S. dollar is tied to the price of crude oil and petroleum production. Because oil producing countries only accept dollars for oil, linking US currency to the commodity maintains the dollar as the world's dominant currency. All currencies throughout the world are nothing more than a promissory note, including the U.S. dollar. As oil producing countries decouple the sale of crude from US currency began to destabilize the dollar making it more akin to Fiat money. Fiat money is government-issued promissory notes, which are not backed by a commodity.

Today, the value of money is derived from its relationship to supply and demand of the government issuing the note. Regardless of the promissory note issuance, capital backed with the strongest currency to finance enterprise expansion or to create new projects is paramount. Wealthy people and large corporations around the world invest in the strongest currency to park their money or raise large sums of capital. In most cases, these same people and corporations help drive bullish markets, and if they fail, their investments are protected to withstand bear market downturns. African Americans suffered from Bubbles, especially during the tech and real estate bust, causing a loss of wealth and land ownership which perpetuated a downward spiral of credit worthiness. African Americans make up three percent of the venture capital investor market, and less than one percent of the $150 billion in venture capital funding is linked to Black company start-ups in 2020 according to a recent study. There are six Black-led Venture Capital Fund Management firms (MAC Venture Capital, Collab Capital, Include Ventures, Fearless Fund, Harlem Capital, and Founders First Capital partners) with $508 million amongst them. What do they bring? According to experts, Americans saving rate as a whole rose across the board by as much as ten percent during the pandemic crisis, but not so much for Black people.

For Minority Depository Institutions (MDI) and their African American depositors, COVID-19 eroded what little savings they had accumulated post the Great Recession 2009. Between 2010 and 2019, the percentage of Black household savings rose thirty-nine percent. Unfortunately, only thirty-five percent of Black households had retirement accounts during the same period. For many wealthy investors and U.S. Corporations in large non-MDI financial institutions like JP Morgan, Bank of America, Wells Fargo, and Citigroup with assets totaling $8.4 Trillion, held on to their cash reserves by forty-eight percent as a percent change over the last ten years, while Black banks made up a small fraction of cash reserves in the U.S. The wealth gap between Whites and Blacks cannot be more illustrative than comparing the total assets of financial institutions across the nation. Most billionaires and millionaires are more likely to use large financial institutions to manage their wealth portfolio, e.g., Bank of America, Citi, Morgan Stanley, and BB&T private client services to name a few. The combined asset of all MDI Black-owned banks totals $6.8 billion in the U.S.: Broadway, $1 billion; Carver State Bank, $700 million; Carver Federal Savings Bank, $687 million; One United Bank, $658 million; First Tuskegee Bank, $600 million; Industrial Bank, $550 million; Citizens Trust Bank, $$429 million; Seaway Bank, $361 million; First Independence Bank, $$256 million; Mechanics & Farmers Bank, $255 million; Liberty Bank & Trust, $230 million; Unity National Bank, $187 million; Tri-State Bank, $110 million; Citizens Bank (Nashville), $109 million; North Milwaukee State Bank, $61 million; United Bank of Philadelphia, $60 million; South Carolina Community Bank, $52 million; Alamerica Bank, $43 million; First State Bank, $37 million; Columbia Savings & Loan, $24 million; The Harbor Bank, $2.1 million, and Commonwealth National Bank, $1.6 million.

As a result of the pandemic, many large financial institutions reduced their brick-and-mortar branches and shifted to online banking services and automatic teller machines (ATM) exclusively. If the core of the bank is to remain a regional player, then the growth model will remain limited to the regional value chain. The real opportunity is to look beyond its regional boundary and consolidate with other regional players to form a more powerful presence. With the infusion of the Bipartisan Infrastructure Law (BIL) financial stimulus and additional backing of deposits from founder's roundtable stakeholders could place Black-owned banks on solid ground. More importantly, it could facilitate a competitive position to increase its capital and enable them to participate in holding corporate and large municipals bonds for industries like airports, airlines, manufacturing, and hospitals. They can also take a more active role in the wealth management space of international and domestic clients, refinance mortgages and offer lines of credit to issuing bank credit cards. The EAC must ensure African Americans can participate in the country's impending infrastructure boom with sustaining income and access to capital. A cash rich banking system will help facilitate investments across multiple sectors where people of color, and Black people, are traditionally under-represented.

Competitors and Technical Challenges

Rounding out the top financial institutions in the United States is Bancorp, Truist Financial Group, PNC, TD Bank, Capital One, and Mellon Bank of NY.

There are many dominant regional non-MDI bank competitors, e.g., just in the Midwest market, includes Citizens Bank ($185 billion), Huntington Bank ($175 billion), Key Bank ($171 billion), Comerica ($88 billion), and TCF ($46 billion), recently purchased by Huntington Bank.

The national and regional banks have the advantage of coverage to transfer accounts, better managed branches and offer a variety of financial services that caters to a broad customer base.

The MDI must overcome the challenge of scale. For example, a new entry Black-owned Atlanta-based Greenwood bank struggled to launch its online platform and automatic teller machine (ATM) network. Venture capitalist like Varo digital banking could offer new avenues for African Americans but separate from MDI banks.

Regulatory and Market Barriers

There are several factors impacting MDIs credit risk and return on investment:

- Professionally Managed Operations
- Trust and Confidence
- Prudent Investments and Wealth Management
- Industry Innovation
- Customer Service

The basis of the African American banking value proposition requires two inputs: 1) it would involve further consolidation amongst Black-owned banks and VCs under the leadership of the founder's roundtable board, and 2) the merger would need approval from the federal regulatory agencies.

The African American Keiretsu Banking System serves as the catalyst for the Conglomerate.

A national African American Keiretsu banking value proposition could facilitate the ability to expand financial markets and exceed real production of the economy and avoid investing in useless things. With the U.S. Congress passage the African American Reparations Act of 2030 recognizes that Black Americans make up twelve percent of the U.S. population and shall direct a proportional percent of the $1.5 trillion BIL or ~$360 billion to be administered through the EAC consolidated banks to invest in the Black communities.

Where will African Americans invest its portion of the BIL?

For the first time in U.S. history, African Americans would be in the position to restore their human infrastructure to rebuild the social fabric of its community; from developing an academic pipeline to business investments that will help advance America's ability to build new urban centers to combat climate change and advance the future of the country – nation building at home.

CHILD DEVELOPMENT & EDUCATION INDUSTRY

One of the greatest challenges for the EAC is to remake education for African Americans, starting with elementary and high schools all the way through college graduation, as well as the reconciliation with religious groups. During the 1980's – 1990's, African Americans lost multiple generations of young people to prisons due to the U.S. governments zero tolerance on crime and drugs policies, resulting in an unprecedented incarceration rate for Black men and Black boys. Sadly, this modern travesty occurred under both political parties; the Reagan Administration (Republican) and the Clinton Administration (Democrat). Today, Black youth are seduced into fast money-making schemes through entertainment or professional sports. Without proper training and education, they are duped into perpetuating gang life and the drug culture through exploitive rap music. Unfortunately, there is a sinister side to the quick pathway to riches and fame under the auspice of signing onto a major music label. The label would advance the artist millions of dollars and encourage them to spend the money on senseless luxury items to promote their fake lavish lifestyle, only to fall in debt to the label. The executives of the label take control of the artist and become the property of the label, selling the brands and the image dictated by the label. It's embarrassing to learn that seventy percent of professional Black athletes lose their wealth a few years after leaving their respective leagues. The EAC must intervene and re-educate the youth and redirect their minds, body, and soul to reach for more rewarding and worthwhile stations to pursue and sustain their lives in the long run. Kindergarten – High School: It's clear that church attendance is falling across all denominations. For Black people, it is problematic because secular training alone could further exacerbate the lack of moral compass of the African American community. The lesson learned from other successful faith-based programs (e.g., Catholic, and Jewish), is they help established academic pipelines to cultivate future leaders. The three most prestigious private high schools (Phillips Academy-Andover, Harvard-Westlake, and Phillips Exeter Academy) are amongst the top academic institutions in the United States. They have tough academic requirements, where SAT scores fall in the ninety-third percentile and a thirteen percent acceptance rate. Coupled with a small student- to-teacher ratio, it is difficult to enroll new students. Other major parochial schools (Friends, Country Day, and Catholic school networks) have high rate of college-bound students too. There are conflicting studies; on one hand, private school students have a five percent higher graduation rate than public schools and are nearly two times likely to apply for secondary education and graduate from a four-year college. Another study by the University of Virginia challenged conventional wisdom that public schools are less effective in educating students than private schools. It really comes down to two things: parental involvement and school management. Because of funding, public institutions like inner city schools are poorly managed, it expands the privatization movement business model but not in a good way. For inner city Black youth, the shift from failing public schools fills the pipeline towards "For Profit" prisons. An African American child development plan must include a prekindergarten (PK) and prekindergarten through fifth grade (pk5) learning system. Utilizing the same strategy as the Jewish and Catholic Archdiocese, African Americans should build on the Isuthu Institute & Intojane Institute concept introduced by the ministry of Fellowship Chapel Church, Detroit, Michigan). Universities: What good is the BIL if Black people are not prepared with the skills and qualifications to participate in it? One of the most significant failures for Black firms is its inability to win government contracts because African American firms lack the minimum qualifications. W.E.B. Du Bois and Booker T. Washington were both correct when they debated the path of Black professions as it was never an either-or argument because Black people needed to learn skilled trades and earn professional degrees. Emphasis must change amongst the Historical Black College and Universities (HBCU) to focus on adult learning & certification and advanced STEM curriculums must include mastering in aerospace & propulsion; architecture, landscape architecture, agriculture & horticulture; astronomy; botany; computer science; construction management; certified public accountant & financial; energy; engineering; geology; healthcare & dietary; MBA Program; medicine; space travel; and skilled trades. The greatest exploitation of Black youth is how major public state universities across the country under the guidance of the NCAA capitalize on elite African American athletes. Black youth, often from poor communities, are recruited to large predominantly White universities where the coaches, often White men, are paid millions of dollars. The HBCU should be vying for a national championship every year and providing their athletes with financial links to their community. Today, Black students are being directed away from studies aimed at critical thinking. The EAC must establish an educational network of institutes that will not only enable Black students to master the SAT standards and an Afrocentric curriculum. African American students should not have their educational knowledge marginalize to Ebonics, but maximized in a way that include Science, Technology, Engineering and Mathematics (STEM) and mastering proper English and other foreign languages to ensure they are prepared academically to apply and compete at any university in America just like they do in sports. Regardless of the race, talent acquisition for millennials will require a different approach; an approach that aligns with their values and the things they're passionate about on a personal level. EAC needs to lead and get into the minds of African American youth while they are young; nurturing them as they grow up; not only the likes of great literature, but through math and science camps so they understand Black businesses are making the investments in them instead of relying on government programs exclusively. How is this possible that poor countries, especially countries in Africa, can produce higher performing students than the U.S.? While there are many reasons for African Americans ranking last amongst other groups, there's no excuse for Black people accepting it!

The African American Academic Pipeline

Competitors and Technical Challenges

The notion that African Americans are inherently incapable of testing at a competitive level is ridiculous. The reason Asians consistently score in the high percentile is their preparation. It comes down to access to resources and encouragement. One important thing to note, Black students drop out of college because they accumulate fifty percent higher debt, while Hispanic accumulate thirty percent and White students, less than twenty percent.

Regulatory & Market Barriers

There are other physical and market barriers. For example, Black students do not have safe environments conducive for learning, support systems in the home, or have access to broadband technology, and resources to attract competent teachers experienced at providing extensive academic material to African American students.

Invest in the African American Academic Pipeline

An investment in the human infrastructure includes the national establishment of the Isuthu Institute to focus on pre-K through 12 educations. Access to quality higher education is paramount. Just enrolling into college is not enough; EAC must produce a culture of early learning focused on skilled trades and professional degrees. The EAC must focus on eliminating African American student loan debt and help create an environment to help educate Black children by providing them with the skills to effectively learn critical thinking and problem solving, as well as prepare these young people with the ability to solve complex issues through engineering, education, mathematics, statistics, and physical sciences, including financial solutions. These future students will be amongst the people to participate and compete for future infrastructure projects.

ENGINEERING, TECHNOLOGY & TRADES INDUSTRY

Mankind has always observed nature and the environment since the Ancient Egyptians who learned how to harness the power of the flooding of the Nile River. History is riddled with examples of learning about catastrophic events; and now it's climate change. Climate change is real, and uncertain as to when the next catastrophic event will happen. Modern people must overcome the inevitability of the next climate phenomenon. The notion of foreign students taking jobs from Americans is a false argument. The fact of the matter is foreign students are being hired for jobs Americans are not qualified to fill. The U.S. had to import foreign computer scientist from India to recruiting other foreign students to advance STEM research at U.S. universities to maintain its high academic standards. To ensure African American firms can participate in large scale infrastructure projects being proposed under the US infrastructure Bill will require more than access to capital. It will require a strong pool of qualified engineers and contractors who meet minimum qualifications. African Americans make up less than two percent of professional engineers in the United States, as companies cannibalize their talent and minimize the strength of Black-owned firms. What are the visionaries thinking as they reimagine an alternative to earth? One alternative is Outer space, which may provide away to overcome the unpredictability of climate change and man-made catastrophes on earth. Less than a decade ago, Space-based industries would have required significant investment to design systems light enough to deploy in outer space and maintain orbiting above the earth's atmosphere. The space race between the USA and USSR started in 1900 and was heavily subsidized by their respective governments. With the commercialization of space flight and multiple launches occurring more frequently has reduced the cost that previously challenged the technology. In 1946, an African American mathematician and physicist, Walter McAfee, calculated the speed of the Moon, and today, one of America's prominent astrophysicist and scientist, Neil deGrasse Tyson, speaks about the importance of space. Now, billionaires have taken over the space industry, where individuals like Elon Musk, Jeff Bezos and Richard Branson have purchased scientists and technology to advance their vision of commercializing space travel. The survival of humans has always relied on our ability to observe nature and learn how to adapt and thrive. The effect of climate change impacts the entire planet and influences how our cities and urban landscape will evolve and accommodate future generations approaching 9.8 billion people. Coal was an abundant source of power that contributed to Carbon Dioxide (CO_2) and global warming. Early developments attempted to explore ways to make clean-coal plants by trapping CO_2 by two billion tons a year. Unfortunately, the first technique reduced plant efficiency by a third and doubled the cost of producing power. Today, scientists want to design coal power plants to burn CO_2 and purified oxygen in the form of compressed metal oxide instead of air, and the plant could capture CO_2 at higher concentration without sacrificing plant efficiency. There are many investment opportunities which the EAC can participate in either through merger or acquisition. With the introduction of production electric vehicles, like the high-end Tesla luxury models, electrified cars have significantly reduced reliance on petroleum-powered mobility. To enhance the electrification market transformation will require better battery technology. For example, better reliability and battery storage capacity, as well as the commercialization and standardization of battery management for homes and transportation. Reducing carbon emission by closing coal plants and replacing them with natural gas and renewable like wind and solar may not be enough and would be short-sighted to omit nuclear energy. The emergence of Smart Cities and Mobility as a Service (MaaS) will present new innovations we only dreamed about as children watching the Jetson cartoons; high-speed rail lines, new airline services connected by vertical-take-off and landing (VTOL) drones to autonomous vehicles, all powered by solid-state electrical motors are possible. People need to understand the use of artificial intelligence and hydrolytic robotics will perform laborious tasks previously done by unskilled laborers. As much as people would like to protect their personal information from hackers, personal and business online transactions alike are unavoidable. Given how much major utility infrastructure and sensitive military systems are integrated to the Internet of Things (IoT) makes the need for cyber security and computer scientist critical to have for the next century. Smart cities will integrate food sources like urban farming supported by green buildings to vertical supply chain, logistic and just-in-time distribution. There are several well-connected government contractors, e.g., Leidos (affiliated with Lockheed), CACI International, Vectrus, and Decisive Date that serve as the HR managers for the federal government. Their demographic looks cookie-cutter, with White males making up over sixty percent of the top decision-making positions. Minorities make up support functions; Blacks (twelve percent) and Hispanics (ten percent) respectively. The same major players like Lockheed Martin, Raytheon, and Northrop Grumman control the military cottage industry, much like large Engineering planning firms who are approved by the federal government to build mega infrastructure projects. There are no comparative African American engineering firms to mention. What is it going to take to approve Black firms to build mega infrastructure projects? The African American academic pipeline must produce more landscape architects, architects, and (civil, chemical, electrical, mechanical, structural, and geological) engineers, with expertise in construction management and cost estimation. What happen to African American artisans? Not everybody will attend college to pursue a professional career, even less likely of becoming professional athletes or entertainers. What is to become of the Black masses? How will they provide for their families and make it possible for their children to aspire to levels beyond their parents? The EAC must bring people together to form a strong workforce model. The number of HVAC technicians, electricians, and pipe fitters, as well as heavy equipment operators are few, but needed to help fortify Black infrastructure builders. The H.J. Russell & Company is an example of what can happen when you match means and technical expertise with appropriate political support. The honorable Maynard Jackson, of Atlanta, GA, hired H.J. Russell & Company to construct a runway at the busiest airport in the United States, Hartsfield-Jackson Atlanta International Airport (ATL), for $172M.

The African American Infrastructure Builders

Competitors and Technical Challenges

Regardless of the infrastructure, from aerospace, cyber security, and autonomous mobility, logistics, and land development, African Americans lag in the capacity to compete.

The major engineering and construction companies (Bechtel, fluor, AECOM, and Jacobs Engineering) are responsible for large-scale infrastructure projects in the U.S. and around the world earn revenues between $10 billion and $26 billion, while the top ten Black engineering and construction firms in the U.S. combined, account for only $112 million.

Other non-Black construction firms in the U.S. includes Kiewit ($8.7 billion), Whiting-Turner ($8.4 billion), Skanska ($7.5 billion), who partnered with Black-owned construction firm, H.J. Russell & Co. PCL ($6.9 billion), Gilbanc ($6 billion), The Walsh Group ($4.8 billion), Belfour Beatty ($4.5 billion), Hensel Phelps ($3.5 billion) and Holdwer ($3.3 billion).

Regulatory and Market Barriers

There are often federal, state, and local procurement ordinances that have significant eligibility hurdles that prevent Black firms to be prime contractors on major contracts:

- Minimum qualifications
- Access and knowledge of Operating Heavy Construction Equipment
- Restricted to the Federal SBA guidelines
- Skilled Trade Pool – Unionized labor groups
- Professional Engineers – Graduation Rates
- Large-scale Infrastructure Experience
- Bond Guarantees
- Insurance

Elon Musk and Jeff Bezos are not aerospace scientists, but both were able to launch successful spacecrafts for commercial use – how did they accomplish such a complicated feat? Concentrated wealth allowed them to hire scientists and influence politicians to remove bureaucratic red tape.

Invest in Training, Hiring, and Promoting African American Infrastructure Builders

African Americans must evolve intellectually and come to terms with their fragmented community to embrace scientific breakthroughs in a way that enables its leaders to advance the lives of Black people. The ability to form consortiums and collaborate is essential. Here's where the foundation and the enterprise come into play to create joint ventures headquartered in regional markets. This will enable them to compete for capital infrastructure projects in the U.S. and around the world. To accelerate the capabilities and capacity needed to compete will require acquisitions and mergers and expand partnerships with established European, Asian, and African firms. This will prove to be the linchpin to enable the conglomerate to penetrate other markets.

FAITH INDUSTRY

The relationship between the education system and one's personal religious beliefs are interwoven. Especially in the modern age, it is indispensably necessary for African Americans to come to terms with interdenominational faith of Black people. Just as the chronicle of African Americans highlighted in the first essay, the religious doctrines of Black people have evolved. Apart from its roots in Africa, in some cases, the enslaved African people were stripped of their language, traditions, and belief systems to become indoctrinated by the religious institutions of their enslavers. Some Afrocentric scholars claim the early Africans were the original Hebrew Israelites (Not affiliated with Orthodox, Conservative, Zionism, Reform or Reconstruction Judaism known today) and amongst early Christianity before the canonicity of the Holy Bible books. Before the Ottman and European conquest, the tribal linguistics and dialects varied across Africa, including ritual beliefs. The Islamic conquerors who invaded northern Africa converted many Africans into Muslims under Sunni or Shia doctrines. It was the influence of Constantine Christianity that gave way to Eastern Orthodoxy, Catholicism and Protestants. During the Colonial Slave Trade, Europeans created colonies in Africa, throughout the Caribbeans, and the United States under the doctrines of the slave masters and Christian missionaries.

Major religions (Islam and Judeo-Christianity) recognize one name, although pronounced and spelled differently amongst them, is Jesus. While there are important differences, they all believe in God, the power of prayer, and charity (European Theologians provided a religious chronicle; e.g.). Judaism gave way to Christianity and the Catholic faith, which split between the Greek (Eastern) Orthodox and Roman Catholic. As Christianity continued to spread across the globe, it did so, fragmenting into various religious denominations. The Protestants broke off from the Roman Catholics. Lutheranism and Calvinism broke away from Protestantism. The Reformed Churches and the Presbyterian Church branched off from Calvinism. From the English Protestants gave way to the Puritans, Separatist and Anglicans; the Puritans joined the Presbyterians. The Separatist formed the Quaker and Baptist and spun off the Disciples of Christ and Churches of Christ while the Episcopal and Methodist branched off from Anglicanism. African Americans were not allowed to worship with slave masters in the U.S. and formed their own branches within European denominations. For example, the African Methodist Episcopal (AME) was founded by an ex-slave, Bishop Richard Allen in 1794 because of racism and discrimination in the church.

In the United States, the trends are alarming to religious institutions as people identifying themselves as Christians found attendance at church service dropping. In 2001, eighty-five percent of people identified as Christians, 2012 (eighty-two percent), 2015 (seventy-one percent), and 2020 (sixty-five percent). Human beings have always had a spiritual connection with a higher power that most people call God. Religion provides spiritual salvation for the soul and gives people security and a sense of belonging through fellowship, as well as an abundance of resources for the collective. Religion serves as an epistemological force in the human psyche. There's an unsavory truth about the faith community, and especially amongst the

Mega Churches and television evangelist that tend to permeate a culture of self-preservation. While these wealthy pastors are considered anointed, they bear much responsibility to the poor congregates to bring resolution and harmony amongst their flock. Some of these religious institutions are leveraging their non-tax status to purchase real estate, start-up businesses and offer services to people in the community, especially education is admirable. Unfortunately, church revenues are skimmed from these various enterprises (music groups, television broadcast and book deals) to enrich the pastor and justified through scripture.

To help fill pews in the church, services are becoming more like entertainment venues that promote everything from concerts and plays to pastoral praise and feel-good allegories. With the advent of American individualism and materialism, African Americans have followed suit in becoming more agnostic and atheist. A small segment of the Black population has sought spirituality and meditation through Hinduism, Buddhism, and Confucianism. The amalgamation of Black people has further splintered the divide amongst African Americans, making the "wealth, political and narrative" construct that much more difficult to achieve. The divide amongst Black people is compounded between the strong conservative views of older African Americans versus the growing younger liberal view who is influence to support homosexuality, multiculturalism, and individual expression. It is not to say these attributes are bad or good, but until there is a renewed moral code for Black people; not just in the United States, but across the globe, outsiders will always influence its belief system. In the matter of leadership, Black men must come to terms with the empowerment of Black women in society and in the church. If there is to be any movement towards reconciliation, Black people cannot continue to operate under a religious theology that divides its people. By embarking on an African American interdenominational faith council could include participation and inclusion of every socio-economic group across all income brackets and racial lines.

The EAC must establish a connection with Black churches of all denominations backed with financial and technical resources, earning their trust, and supporting the needs of their communities. The growth and development of Black children starts the moment they leave their mother's womb and providing early education (pk-12) with the skills to view learning as a lifelong process is critical to change the culture.

The African American Interdenominational Faith Council

Competitors & Technical Challenge

The competition for private schools in the Black community doesn't exist. If Black students have an opportunity to attend a prestigious private school, it comes through scholarships, most likely to play sports.

A challenge for the many Black families is they cannot afford to send their children to private or parochial schools (e.g., Catholic, Jewish and Montessori schools).

Black student with strong academics may be able to attend a so-called Charter (magnet) school, within the public school system. Many highly intelligent black students are lost in the system and overlooked.

Another challenge for the average Black student is the need to have a safe, healthy, and supportive environment that encourage and reinforce a high-level of learning.

Having a well-funded early learning institution designed to cultivate minds spiritually and academically; thus, preparing them to compete at the highest standards in the world is essential. Because Christians, Jewish, and Muslims faiths are organized and unified, they have strong influence over their communities.

Regulatory & Market Barriers

The separation of church and state is as ongoing debate amongst Americans. U.S, churches enjoy the ability to collect money tax-free. The danger during the participation versus isolation period, disenfranchised Black people and poor White people live in prolong isolation, creating an environment for fringe charismatic leaders to distort the teachings of the faith with more radical elements. Black people must recognize and rule out those zealots amongst the fringe independent religious groups that might not be in the best interest of the masses. African American churches must overcome its chiefdoms and build upon a central operating organization like an African American Interdenominational Faith Council to pool its resources to form and broaden the Isuthu (male) and Intojane (female) concept.

Facilitate an African American Interdenominational Faith Council

The African American Interdenominational Faith Council could be away to provide common ground and purpose. The varying religious affiliations amongst African Americans need not divide its people but draw them closer coalescing under a common set of core values. Building on a common belief system will earn trust and build confidence amongst Black people throughout the world. The trust will extend beyond personal beliefs and into how African Americans marry, buy their homes, raise, and educate their children. To conquer the big things, Black people need to conquer the small things first. Finding a way to organize is a seemingly small thing for most groups, but it's huge for African Americans. If Black people can find common ground to build a stable belief system, it will yield an educational pipeline with unlimited potential.

POLITICS & GOVERNANCE INDUSTRY

There is no such thing as a utopia. Dating back to the Paleolithic, Mesolithic, and Neolithic periods, which encompasses pre-historic times to the Golden Age of the Great Nubian and Egyptian empires. And later, followed by the Silver Age of Mesopotamia, and Greek Bronze Age to the Roman Iron Age, humans had conflict. Throughout human history civilizations have waged war against one another, annexed foreign territories, enslaved other people, and exploited the natural resources for the benefit of the ruling empire. Societies continued their exploits through the Industrial, Coal & Petroleum Age, Atomic Age, Nuclear Age and now an emerging Space Age. New empires will rise, and older empires will decline. It comes down to the knowledge, behavior, and beliefs of the people. It is not the position of this paper to answer the question should Black people stay in America or move to another country? However, if the choice is to remain in America, then African Americans must accept American values and find harmony to shape its ethos. Regardless of your political affiliations, Black people should embrace the ideas of American patriotism. The policymakers we elect, must be accountable to Black people. While it is vital to have the ability to influence behavior, control resources, and govern by the rule of law, it needs to be open and fair. The primary power brokers in the United States are a minority group of White men. With nearly ninety-seven percent of Republican elected officials are White, seventy-seven percent of them are White men. Nearly seventy-six percent of Democrats are White men even though White men comprise only thirty-one percent of the US population. In state houses across the country, decisions that impact most people rest in the hands of predominantly White male millionaire policymakers. A large population of African Americans once supported the Republican Party, following the Proclamation of Emancipation under President Abraham Lincoln (#16) up to President Theodore Roosevelt (#26). After the implementation of the southern strategy, poor White southerners and most Black people switched sides. The old Andrew Jackson Dixiecrats became Goldwater Republicans while Black Conservatives became John F. Kennedy Democrats. Neither party offered African Americans full access to power, not even during and after the Obama Presidency. Unfortunately, many Black politicians are seen as modern-day house Negroes holding the keys to the plantation to keep the rest of the Black folks in their place.

The only way to sustain political movements for Black people must include a plan for strong and stable institutions governed by accountable leaders who operate under an agreed upon social doctrine embraced by all Americans. The coalesces of Black politics is essential, as the United States and Western Europe become more populated with immigrants of color has given rise to White Nationalism. It is commonplace for alliances to form between White extremist in the west and White extremist in eastern communist countries like Russia and Hungary. The EAC and its subsidiaries have an ethical and moral obligation to avoid controversy. How we choose to live will drive our actions as a society. If Black people want to participate in the American political hierarchy means African Americans must be prepared to face criticism for supporting past and future geo-political policies stemming from, historical acts of atrocities, unpopular war campaigns to weighing in on new military theaters. The Group of Seven (G7) countries defined as advanced economies, which includes Canada, Germany, France, Italy, UK, Japan, and the United States support the UN Security Council. Corporations (e.g., Lockheed-Martin, Boeing, Northrop Grumman, Raytheon, and General Dynamic) provide one-third of the world's military weapons, grossing $164 billion in revenues. The G7, except for Japan, make up the North Atlantic Treaty Organization (NATO) formed in 1949. The NATO countries' efforts to improve the coordination of economic policy through the International Monetary Fund and World Trade Organization created the expanded Group of Twenty (G20) countries to help govern the global economy. In addition to the G7, the G20 includes Argentina, Australia, Brazil, China, India, Indonesia, Mexico, Saudi Arabia, South Africa, South Korea, Russia, and Turkey. The effect of climate change impacts the entire planet and certain members of the G7 and G20 countries are the largest contributors of carbon emissions. Whether its Russia, Saudi Arabia, the US and Africa, major oil producers around the world are notorious for burning off natural gas (a process known as "Flaring"). In Africa alone, about one-third of its crude-oil extractions account for 40 million tons of CO_2 emission annually. Unemployment in sub-Saharan African countries is a breeding ground for new militant groups who direct their attacks against oil companies by stealing hydrocarbons from pipelines and selling it as inexpensive fuel for generators. It's shameful that some oil rich African countries with vast deposits of crude have succumbed to corruption and greed while its citizens live in poverty. The social responsibility discussion as it relates to the toll on human life is real. The decision to invest in a particular sector or firm has financial and political ramifications. Closer to home, sometimes the decision to invest in a single source provider could supplant one company over another. It's amazing how large cities use the same developers consistently securing billions of dollars in contracts from the federal government to fund mega-projects, creating winners and losers. Who makes these decisions? Who decides the winner and losers? For the most part, people go into politics to do the right thing and to be of service. Unfortunately, some become seduced by the power and lose sight of their mission of goodwill. For there to be a long-sustaining social and political movement for African American reparations and reconciliation, the United States of America must agree to a social contract with the American people. African American leaders should be working to find ways to reduce poor air quality and noise pollution to enhancing urban community developments, combined with affordable housing and good jobs. The EAC must consolidate its fragmented community to promote economic equality and environmental sustainability through public policies and political influence.

The African American Political Alliances

Competitors and Technical Challenges

There are competing interests across the political spectrum, and it's important to understand their position. These powerful foundations support certain voting blocs, political parties, and interest groups. They may or may not have African American's best interest:

- CPAC – Conservative Political Action Committee
- American Enterprise Institute – Conservative Research ($111M)
- Heritage Foundation – Conservative Research ($80M)
- Brookings Institute – Liberal Research ($355M Endowment)
- Carnegie Endowment – International Peace ($46M)
- CATO Institute – Libertarian Beliefs
- Rand Corporation – Federally and State Research: Health and Security
- Federal Society – Law and Public Policies
- Pulse Institute – Social and Economic Issues
- NAACP – Legal Justice
- National Action Network (NAN) – Fight for Social Injustice

Some think tanks' special interest groups are funded by wealthy donors, like CPAC to help drive conservative outcomes. The foundation supported by the EAC must draft legislation to support the kind of laser focus policies and regulations to facilitate growth in its communities.

Regulatory and Market Barriers

For decades, the U.S. Government has decided how many immigrants are allowed into the country and what industry they can participate. The Black community served as the consumer for these new immigrants, expanding their wealth and political influence at the expense of African Americans. Other political barriers:

- Congressional Maps and Gerrymandering
- Hired Lobbyist
- Gentrification
- Federal Regulations and Compliance bureaucracy
- Foreign Money
- White Nationalism
- Misinformation
- Political Corruption

Through its money and analytics, the foundation must influence the outcomes to overcome the above-mentioned issues to help provide favorable policies to support Black industries and the quality of life for working poor (Black and White) communities.

Establish an African American Political Alliances

It's not enough for the Black geo-political agenda to be limited to protecting people against social issues and promoting good education. The EAC must use its wealth to change public policies, or Black people will continue to be depicted as disorganized subjugated people victimized by police brutality and Black on Black crimes. Who wants to be affiliated with such a weak group of people? The foundation must demand effective governance; not limited to the status quo, religious or political affiliation and geographical boundaries. The foundation must represent the ultimate form of advocacy for the American people. African Americans are not monolithic, no more than Asians, Europeans, and Middle easterners, and yet these other groups find a way to organize amongst themselves and influence others to their side. Even people of the Jewish, Catholic, and Muslim faith do not vote the same way, unless it's a matter of public policies affecting their wealth, religion, and communities, as they unanimously hold their elected officials accountable. African Americans must vote to support their own best interest as a whole or risk further weakening its political clout.

WORK, LEISURE & NARRATIVE INDUSTRY

African Americans work life and leisure must be in balance with its purpose; as they create wealth and develop political alliances, the EAC must also steer its people towards good moral character. There is no denying the natural laws of science, which explain the physical constraints of gravity and matter through physics, chemistry, and other scientific disciplines. It would be disingenuous on the part of the EAC to ignore spiritual laws, for those people who accept God's covenant and rely on God's grace. As human beings, we have a set of psychological hierarchy of our needs. According to renowned psychologist, Abraham Maslow, clothing, food, and shelter make up basic human needs. The simple truth for most people is about having a good job to provide for your family and the ability to provide housing and security and prosper. Even though homeownership has always been limited in the Black community, there was a time when African Americans owned and operated farms, hospitals and insurance companies that served its community. We all have the need to be loved and belong, which focuses on relationships and a sense of connectivity. For many years, Black churches, barber shops and salons once served in this capacity, but are now being replaced with social media. We have a need for self-esteem, which today is often associated with education, money, and fame. Many Black people have acclaimed recognition for producing great academic work, amassing great wealth, and achieving great athletic heights. Unfortunately, they are always under pressure for being the first Black, or the only Black to represent the entire race. Their notoriety is always under scrutiny and any indiscretion is seen as a reflection of all Black people. While it is impossible to be Jesus, aspiring to be self-actualized with high moral standards should be the goal. African Americans must use their talents to help others, the ultimate level is transcendence, and living in accordance with a higher power, or however one defines it. Passing these beliefs onto the masses beyond the church has always existed. For example, the theater has been a large part of shaping human experience since ancient times. For decades, publications, television, movies, and now the internet help shape public opinion, usually with unflattering stereotypes of Black people; from misrepresenting their true connections with ancient empires like Egypt and Nubia, instead, showing films like "Tarzan", "Gone with the Wind", "Uncle Tom's Cabin", "Black Exploit Films", "Roots" to "Django Unchained"). Black people attempted to establish media platforms to combat these stereotypes only to succumbed to market pressures due to weak programming or were acquired by larger media outlets. Even some Black people reinforced these stereotypes, especially comedians. WZZM 13 and WGPR Channel 62 were amongst the first Black television stations in the United States started in Detroit, Michigan. Another well-known Black media outlet, Black Entertainment Television (BET) Network was sold to Viacom for $3 billion, making Robert Johnson the first African American billionaire. Jet Magazine and later Essence Magazine declined like other print media. The EAC could utilize the power of computer-generated imagery (CGI) and Pixar like animation technology to create epic motion pictures to reenact African history. Whose idea was it to create the narrative "Defund the Police"? Why not, "Make-Police-Better!" "Black Lives Matter" is a true statement, but if the appeal is for all Americans and people around the world to embrace the cause, why not "All Lives Matter"? Both marketing campaigns failed miserably. The powerful people who control the national narrative did achieve their goal, however, by creating false arguments meant to divide the people – mission accomplished! How do we, as a society, pivot from the current trajectory of separate and opposing universes of thought? Elon Musk is an example of what one person can do to change the narrative landscape. He recently purchased the social media platform, Twitter, for $43 billion. While it's not clear about Mr. Musk politics, clearly, he appears to be a believer of science having launched Space-X. He should also serve as an example to wealthy Black people, demonstrating how wealth can influence the type of politics to control your own narrative. Social media continues to play a huge role in shaping people's opinions. Even former President Trump is getting in on the action, launching "Truth Social". The top online social media platforms are Facebook (ninety-three percent). Twitter (seventy-nine percent), LinkedIn (seventy-five percent), Google (fifty-six percent), YouTube (fifty-five percent), Pinterest (forty-five percent), Instagram (thirty-six percent), Side Share (fifteen percent), Forum (fourteen percent), Social reviews (e.g., YELP thirteen percent), Subscriptions (e.g., REDDIT nine percent), Geo-Locations (five percent), and Snap Chat (two percent). All the top platforms were developed in Silicon Valley near the San Francisco Bay area. Social media platforms have proven to foster misinformation echo-chambers and groupthink that is polarizing the country. The EAC could seize the opportunity to create new social media content to change the opinions of the masses in a more organic and meaningful way and help drive a purpose for living for the American people to combat stereotypes.

The African American Secular Social Norm

<u>Competitors and Technical Challenges</u>

If Black people don't find a way to promote their own story and what they represent as a people, someone else will do it for them. It will not be easy for African Americans to penetrate the mass media market.

The EAC must overcome the powerful algorithms of Silicon Valley that drive advertisement dollars. The top ten global media powerhouses listed early control the mass media space.

Successful Black franchises like "Power", Tyler Perry's Medea", and programs like "Our Kind of People" and "Insecure" have had much appeal. However, to change the mindset will require epic movie productions and high-quality journalism presented in a compelling and meaningful manner.

With the advancement of virtual technology could level the playing field and allow Black media platforms to deploy its stimulating content globally and redefine African American patriotism.

The power of metadata, artificial intelligence, computer-generated imagery (CGI), embedded body camera apparel, and touchless interactive virtual reality will create the next generation of human interactions.

The content delivery mechanism: from television monitors, cell phones, automobiles to laptop computers will be obsolete and replaced by virtual systems will become commonplace.

Regulatory and Market Barriers

What will it take to create a new mass media market? Utilize the foundation's policy arm to ensure it meets all the federal compliance requirements with the Federal Communications Commission (FCC).

The EAC must overcome misinformation amongst the Truth War. What will it take to earn the trust of the masses? The EAC must build consensus about information truthfulness and worthiness by engaging people directly in a responsible way.

Reshape the African American Secular Social Norms

Establishing a new African American ethos is another example where acquisitions and mergers will accelerate visioning needed to effectively course correct the Black narrative. This should serve as part of the building blocks to change global perception and shift public opinion. The enterprise will enable the diversity of the conglomerate to expand into the global media market tied to the purpose for living under the Customer Experience as a Service (CEaaS) umbrella.

In this case, African Americans must restore integrity and trustworthiness of information and create a new narrative of American Exceptionalism that includes the contribution of all Americans. The EAC will reimagine the ideals of America and make the case for American exceptionalism 2.0.

NEXT STEPS

To use the analogy "You can break a single straw easily, but when you bundle straws together, they become seemingly unbreakable", holds true for people too. If African Americans were united, they could become an extremely strong group. It begins with creating a formidable company capable of competing and penetrating new markets. To accomplish such a feat Black people must be willing to cooperate and collaborate with one another across the country, and in some cases, around the world. The reparation template requires strategizing, planning, and organizing to execute at all socio-economic levels. One might ask why the markets can't work more like sporting events where the action of the players is governed by the rules of the game. Well, it is, and it's called regulations, statutory compliance, and ordinances. Despite all the rules to provide oversight of the market in the real world, it still comes down to the people with no instant reply to right the wrongs. We're left with an array of opaque processes, in which wealth, power and political influence pick the winners and losers. The foundation must work to build a tangible African American community, referred to as the Basecamp. The Basecamp would be a place recognized around the world as the center of wealth, commerce, political influence, and moral consciousness for African Americans. The elusive Basecamp is at the core of economic wealth for Black people and the basis of building political power to ensure key decision-makers are held accountable to their constituents. African Americans must seize control of real property to attract a new breed of citizenry to the Black community to spur economic independence and prosperity. Through entrepreneurship and market innovation, African Americans can foster new brands, products, and service opportunities. Black people must make a fundamental shift in the way they interact, exchange ideas, and engage with one another across the socio-political landscape. While past strategies were appropriate and necessary during their formation, history has shown that reliance on singular organizations like the NAACP, the Black Urban League, fraternities, sororities, and other standalone organizations are not enough. Black people need to form a foundation that interconnect its people in a more coordinated and inclusive manner. If Black people are unable to successfully insulate their leaders from distortion, it will weaken the lines of succession and make the organization vulnerable and diminishes the effectiveness of the EAC over time. The EAC leadership must harness and protect the brainpower and ingenuity of liked-minded individuals capable of delivering real results in the long-run. It's not about simply consolidating investors, the EAC must have the imagination and vision to unify Black people around a common plan, garner support from the legislature and sustain commitment from the American people. Impossible? Unrealistic? Accepting these false obstacles is a declaration of defeat, helplessness, and victimization. Being a victim is now a choice and should never be an option. To become victorious is to proclaim self-determination in the face of overwhelming odds. The only limitation for African Americans is self-imposed! Black people are leaving major cities in huge numbers, not seen since the Great Migration. The reasons are the same, in search of the "American Dream", where anyone, regardless of their origin or class can achieve success, and for Black people, means good jobs, safe neighborhoods, and upward mobility for their children. Unfortunately, Black people still face racial profiling and discrimination. This should be a reminder to Black people they should stop running behind other people and create their own community. You can take a Black person out of a community, but you can't take the Black experience out of the person – until Black people face their own unity issues, they will always fall apart no matter how much money they have or where they live because the stereotypes that defined African Americans will always follow them.

THE BASECAMP

I believe the African American journey is akin to the biblical portrayal of the Jews, after 400 years of bondage in Egypt. The Jewish diaspora sought new land across the Jordan River into the promised land of Canaan. African Americans must learn from the great triumphs of the past. Many cultures dispersed from around the world and immigrated to America to establish their communities, and the American people eventually came to accept them. These new immigrants formed strong unified communities across America, and now, Black people must come to terms with the inevitability that challenges its security. There will always be a mantra of "No justice – No peace" until African American detach from its Nomads-like moniker and build a tangible community of landowners. The coronavirus pandemic (COVID-19) took the year of 2020 by storm. The effects of the pathogen devastated the world's economy. The impact on African Americans, which make up approximately twelve percent of the population in the U.S. had the highest level of unemployment and suffered disproportionately higher percent (forty – seventy percent) of deaths amongst those state's hardest hit by the virus. Economists from the International Monetary Fund (IMF) believe the recovery from the pandemic will take many years. The World Health Organization (WHO) and the Center for Disease Control (CDC) expects the disease to remain with us indefinitely as part of life, managed by using effective vaccines to stabilize global herd immunity. Human beings depend on its ability to survive and endure catastrophic forces, whether they are natural or man-made as we learned through trial and error how to protect lives and improve the conditions of society by advancing our knowledge and developing new ways to maintain our existence. African Americans must own land and develop it as they see fit. The only way Black people can build its own community will require a collection of educated, intelligent, and determined people with the means and political clout to achieve it.

THE BASECAMP

- PREFACE
- INTRODUCTION
- COMMUNITY DEVELOPMENT
- THE CITY OF DETROIT PROPOSAL

PREFACE

During the post Emancipation era, you may recall Marcus Garvey wanted to establish a new government in Africa led by Black people, and some blacks agreed. The U.S. government eventually installed the country of Liberia in western Africa, but most Blacks did not move. During the early 1970's, there was a failed attempt by a Pan-African Separatist Movement to bring forth an argument for installing a provisional government for Black people within the borders of the United States, called the Republic of New Africa (RNA); a so-called black belt (territory stretching from Maryland to Arkansas) led by self-proclaimed non-U.S. citizen Black nationalist. I have always challenged this notion as being misguided and illogical, which is why the concept never materialized. While the RNA's disputes against the government for supporting systemic racism and discriminatory policies were valid, the idea of seceding from the United States and embracing Marxism as a form of governance was and is untenable. Nevertheless, the idea of a Basecamp is important, and to achieve the Basecamp in a way that the American people will accept, and the world will recognize, is to earn it out right and in the open. I maintain the same arguments throughout the MEAC; build wealth; influence politics to demand changes to public policies. And then create a legacy for future generations. The prerequisite to the MEAC is to organize, plan, and then execute! I applaud famous people like Sean (Diddy) Combs, Michael Reeder (aka, Killer Mike), LeBron James, and Pharrell Williams and other Black celebrities and activists who used their platform to help the Black community. I hope they join the conversation because Black people need them. No matter how hard they try to go alone, it will have little impact to move the masses. To change the consciousness of Black people will require more than a few famous people with good intentions. I understand it can be frustrating to work with others, especially those with big personalities, and who perhaps are richer than you. I assure you, there's no escaping the need for like-minded Black people to unite African Americans under the right circumstances. The actions of outsiders have created superficial Black folklores and manufactured negative narratives about Black people that is inconsistent with their own core beliefs. Unfortunately, some Black people have become implicit in spreading these false rumors because Black people lack the ability to combat a counter argument. These powerful outsiders' prey upon the poorly educated and weak-minded of the proverbial Black community (rich and poor people alike) to produce misinformation causing outrageously immoral behavior. The dispersion of Black people across the Americas stemming from the trans-Atlantic Slave Trade had to live with institutionalize racism and housing discrimination across the African diaspora. An important argument of the MEAC is the building of a truly physical African American community; designed, built, and managed by Black people. I think the city of Detroit, Michigan could be an excellent test-case for African American reparations administered through the African American Infrastructure roadmap. I'll give a detailed account in this paper.

If you do not agree with Detroit as the test case, then simply replace Detroit with another urban center because the approach remains the same with some natural resource constraints and technical variations. The strategy is to package an urban infrastructure plan that can be replicated and implemented across the country. The foundation will provide the governance and the enterprise will provide the financial support to restore and sustain the Black community. Perhaps Detroit, Michigan could be the epicenter, or Atlanta, Georgia. Both cities have dominant populations of African Americans and both cities have a rich history. The city of Atlanta is at the center of the south and provides products and services to the largest concentration of African Americans in the country. There is no denying that the south remains embroiled in the legacy of the Confederacy and a connection to the bondage of slavery. Despite its history, we have seen much success for Black people in the city of Atlanta, and that progress must continue to flourish. Black people must remain mindful of the pitfalls of paralysis by analysis that could prevent the process from starting. This is not the time to compare and rank one Black organization or one city over another, since it is important to note Black people must harness <u>all its factions</u>. The city of Detroit infrastructure plan is at the heart of the African American reparations for this scenario. The physical and functional act of owning, building, and managing the infrastructure should never be outsourced to another country, but to provide job opportunities for all people living in the greater Detroit area. The Basecamp is about devising new strategies and tactics required to achieve the ultimate outcome, packaging an infrastructure plan, and mobilizing it as a "strategic roadmap" for African Americans across the country. The role of cities with large populations of Black people like the city of Atlanta must continue to serve as the proving ground and litmus test to help shape African American public opinions. For example, how are Black businesses, brands, products, and services viewed around the country? To what extent are African Americans engaged in the national conversation? It is important for the foundation to facilitate lifestyle changes for Black people to create a positive image, while in the background, galvanizing synergies amongst the founder's roundtable to help develop the plan to amass capital, consolidate corporations and franchises to facilitate the redistribution of wealth within the Black community. To make the case for the EAC to become the next group of industrialists in the U.S. will require the ability to think big and invest on a large-scale. I am suggesting the city of Detroit as the business case. The EAC must start with neighborhood properties, and later close the gap of properties surrounding Midtown and Downtown. African Americans must remain humble, honest, and always try to do the right thing. Remember, this national conversation with the American people about is doing the right thing and promoting the American dream for all.

INTRODUCTION

As the world economies reopen from the coronavirus crisis, everyone is looking for new opportunities. Whether we like it or not, life will change, and the advancement of new technology will drive new community development models. To recap the previous writing, the foundation outlined the need for Black American unification and reparations and a proposed African American Infrastructure Bill as an instrument to administer it. The enterprise discussed the organizational structure and access to capital needed to facilitate the vision, mission, and profitability to support Black institutions. The Markets went further suggesting new products and services African Americans could invest in as part its human infrastructure. And now the Basecamp will examine a business case for implementing reparations. Without rehashing U.S. history of injustices, the city of Detroit, like most northern cities during the great African American migration was not very welcoming to Black people, as they faced joblessness, housing discrimination and segregation of public facilities. Despite the challenges, early Black Detroiters still managed to piece together a vibrant community with more than 300 businesses known as Paradise Valley. The eastside business district also referred to as Black Bottom, was where Black people owned drug stores, night clubs, restaurants, and salons amongst other businesses, and now they do not exist. When you think of urban renewal development projects in Detroit, Paradise Valley conjures negative sentiments that perpetuated racial polarization between Whites and Blacks for generations. It started with the construction of Interstate 75, which went through the heart of the Black Bottom community. The construction of I-75 all but crushed and annihilated the Black business district; the remnant of a lasting reminder of the disfranchisement of early Black people who settled into the area. The actions of the city planners sent a shockwave of violence and resentment still felt by descendants of residents who still live in Detroit.

As White residents left the city for the suburbs, Detroit became a Black city and saw the election of its first African American mayor, Coleman A. Young, a former Tuskegee Airman. Even under Mayor Young and Highland Park's mayor, Robert Blackwell, the region continued to hemorrhage wealthy residents and political influence, as well as suffered from a barrage of negative media coverage. With the influx of outside capitalist, the city saw new urban development projects, like the Renaissance Center, Hart Plaza, and the Washington Trolley Plaza, all focused on downtown while the neighborhoods continued to decline from poverty, gang violence, petty crimes, illegal drugs, urban blight and reduced public services. The city of Detroit once ranked amongst the top 10 cities in the United States in terms of population, with more than 1.8 million people in 1950, just behind New York, Los Angeles, Chicago, and Houston. By 2008, the population in Detroit fell below 900,000 people. As a result of White flight, systemic racism, corporate greed, compromised politicians, and clergy, as well as misguided labor unions led the city into decay and economic isolation. Like other urban cities whose complexion changed, caused the population shift to the suburbs, leaving little resources for the poor and unorganized minority groups left behind. Over the last four decades, people from Middle Eastern, Pakistanis and India are making their presence known, supplanting the influence of Black residents. While several more African Americans became mayor (Dave Bing, Dennis Archer Sr. and Kwame Kilpatrick) of Detroit, unfortunately they did little to raise the standard of living for Black people or advance a political agenda to benefit Black residents in a meaningful way. Under their leadership produced further reduction of its population, tax base, and public services. The city suffered from alleged corruption and mismanagement that led to the first bankruptcy of a major city in U.S history, forcing the State of Michigan to appoint a city manager to administer the bankruptcy process and spawn a surge of gentrification. As in most large cities, prominent individuals, families, and corporations help to define the city's vision and politics, like new outsider, Dan Gilbert, an American businessman, investor, and co-founder of Quicken Loan. Mr. Gilbert saw a great opportunity and made good on his investment in Detroit, as he purchased property in downtown Detroit, controlling fifty-one percent of the city's core real estate. Under his property development and management firm (Bedrock), spearheaded a new wave of gentrification in Detroit. Given Mr. Gilbert's health and wellbeing, one might ask how long will his plan last and who will follow him? Prominent individuals, families, and corporations also help define the city through philanthropy. The city of Detroit power players includes the Ford Family, owners of Detroit Lions NFL Team; the Ilitch Family, owner of Detroit Tigers MLB Team and Detroit Red Wings NHL Team; and Penske Family, sponsors of the Detroit Grand Prix all focused on downtown Detroit, via the Detroit Riverfront Conservancy (DRC), the Downtown Development Authority (DDA), and the Detroit Economic Growth Corporation (DEGC) clearly to protect their investments. Imagine if Africans and African American billionaires took advantage of the opportunity by investing in urban developments on a large scale. The MEAC is proposing the establishment of the city of Detroit Infrastructure Plan Authority (DIPA) and position the EAC to administer an infrastructure plan that focuses, initially, on the city of Detroit neighborhoods and adjacent suburbs to create a new pathway of economic investment and community development. By acquiring land, reimagining abandoned office spaces, and rebranding the neighborhood marketplace and reverse the gentrification process and reclaim the city of Detroit power base. The transformational partnership between the enterprise and the city's municipality will launch one the most comprehensive neighborhood reconstruction plan in U.S. history. The goal is to attract young (Black, White, and international) entrepreneurs back to the city to create the momentum needed to control the Basecamp through land ownership. Once the city of Detroit residence assumes its stronghold on the political system, the growth in population will force demand for upstream services like public transportation, public parks and public safety, and water and sanitary infrastructure, as well as construction management and local trades. The next step in the process is to turn attention to childcare, child development, mental health, and education, food sources, as well as a dietary program. The African American Infrastructure Bill, via the city of Detroit Infrastructure Plan gives America an opportunity makes good on its promise that all people have the inalienable right to pursue happiness, and therefore, will no longer interfere with the progress, and allow a tangible black community to take shape. If African Americans are allowed to flourish, the city will naturally evolve organically to reflect the growth and maturity of its mosaic black heritage, culture, and diversity.

COMMUNITY DEVELOPMENT

There's no disputing the progress made under current Mayor Mike Duggan's leadership, and the local power brokers who support him. While the mayor's efforts have similar characteristics outlined in the MEAC, the EAC is focused more with African Americans investing in each other. It is here where the EAC has an opportunity to utilize value innovation to reimagine the city of Detroit identity as the new mecca of commerce, technology, geopolitical center, and social renaissance for African Americans. Do not confuse community development like those sponsored by government entitlements. Community Development, used here, is about nation building at home, building a community infrastructure, for example, public service infrastructure, economic infrastructure, and people infrastructure. There should be no mistake that when people own their land and property, they treat it differently. And land ownership provides access to capital and credit unlike renters and squatters. No matter how many urban section-eight housing projects are constructed for poor people, they will never appease African Americans who seek reparations, as these projects only prolong a slave mindset of dependency and victimization.

THE ROLE OF THE FOUNDATION

With the backing of a strong consolidated national African American Keiretsu (AAK) banking system, the foundation will have access to sufficient capital to make significant investments to finance the Detroit Infrastructure plan. The foundation will preemptively work to prepare an interdenominational summit with major religious faiths in the greater Detroit Metropolitan area to engage the clergy and congregations as to how they can help achieve unification and reconciliation in the region. Assuming successful progress of the African American Reparations Act of 2030 and the appropriations of the African American Infrastructure Bill, the foundation will bring credibility, responsibility, and accountability for all funding audit matters, using the city of Detroit Infrastructure plan as the test case for all subsequent proposals. An important outcome of the reparations passage is the legal formation of the city of Detroit Infrastructure Plan Authority

(DIPA). The foundation will take the lead in presenting the proposal to the United States Congress, the State of Michigan Economic Development Corporation (MEDC), Wayne County government, and to the Detroit city council outlining the municipality and public private partnership (PPP) cooperatives similar to the Wayne State University (WSU) economic development in Midtown and the New Center area designed to implement and administer a broader regional proposal that aligns with the Detroit Regional Partnership (DRP) and Regional Transportation Authority (RTA). Because DIPA is a quasi-public entity, the organization make-up will be comprised of publicly appointed directors to manage the procurement process. A newly proposed Universal Procurement Ordinance (UPO) is essential to ensure the selection of qualified African American contractors who meet the minimum standards and certification requirements. The UPO does not preclude participation of non-African Americans to compete for infrastructure contracts but incentivizes traditional power players in the industry to proactively seek out partnerships to create strong business synergies to competitively bid for new contracts administered through DIPA. While the federal government can impose certain requirements to assure adherence and access to funding, the State of Michigan must authorize the Authority's Board governance in the state. At the end of the day, it is up to the discretion of the MEDC how capital project funding is appropriated across the state.

THE DETROIT INFRASTRUCTURE PLAN AUTHORITY (DIPA)

The first order of business is to enact, ratify and appoint the seven-member Detroit Infrastructure Plan Authority (DIPA) board in the State of Michigan, and subsequent process for the appointment of its members. Regardless of the state, the standard proposed seven-member board shall be appointed as shown below. The rationale is to ensure a balance of power regardless of which party controls the White House and the state houses.

- President of the United States Cabinet Secretary of HUD (two appointments)
- Governor of the State (two appointments)

- County Commissioner Executive (one appointment)
- Mayor of the City (one appointment)
- City Council President (one appointment)

The foundation must ensure transparent processes are upheld, especially at the county and city government level. It is critical to establish an effective balanced agenda between business goals and objectives and cultivate community outcomes consistent with the foundation's mission. Ruling out corruption and local political interference is paramount to the success of African American reparations, and the promise to the American people to account for funding.

UNIVERSAL PROCUREMENT ORIDANCE (UPO)

The UPO is an innovative approach to changing the way African Americans can participate in the U.S. Infrastructure Bill. The UPO is of higher standard of scrutiny, such that, the ratified board must establish and adhere to the following governing principles:

- Regular meeting; and include provisions for special meetings
- System of Accounting
- Reports
- Bond Governance
- Conduct Audits (Audit Committee)
- Independent Certified Public Accounting
- Contract Policies and Procedures
- Contract Terms and Conditions
- Appointment and Compensation of the DIPA director
- Duties and Responsibilities of DIPA directors
- Conflict of Interest
- Ethics
- Diversity and Inclusion

The contract award recommendations are based on fully vetted and transparent organizations recognized by the government, state, and local municipalities; including the federal government, State of Michigan MEDC, private construction industry and citizens employed by contractors who were registered and certified in the State of Michigan, Wayne County, and various authorities in the region, are included in the DIPA preferred contractor database.

THE ROLE OF THE ENTERPRISE

Assuming the foundation is successful in recruiting enough like-minded Africans and African American billionaires to form the Emerging American Capitalist (EAC) conglomerate, where various, Black-led corporations will join forces to penetrate the market segments mentioned earlier to produce new brands and products, as well as new services resulting from mergers and acquisitions, including well-known franchise opportunities.

These enterprises will work in conjunction with DIPA to prepare the proposed city of Detroit Master Plan framework by marketing directly to investors, franchises, financiers, and lending institutions, which includes a rapid value assessment to determine value innovation opportunities and potential industry disrupters to create new space in the market.

These enterprises will preemptively work to prepare career development, job training and job placement by marketing to the greater Detroit Metropolitan area in preparation of the skilled workers needed to implement the infrastructure plan and create a "Manage-to-Own" business opportunity amongst members of the targeted community. The talent acquisition ranges from senior management and leadership to store managers and operations personnel.

These enterprises will concurrently prepare direct correspondence to conduct outreach with city of Detroit and adjacent suburban residents to solicit their input how to implement to targeted communities with improved attributes like a community marketplace, parks, transportation hubs, standardize rezoning, schools, and housing, as well as sequencing and timeline. Every neighborhood will establish its own identity that includes a thriving and sustaining community market place. These enterprises will be tasked with the following responsibilities associated with drafting and implementing the Master Plan Framework:

- Provide strategic visioning to state and city officials through stakeholder engagement
- Provide an EAC firm to facilitate designs of individual community master plans
- Incorporate existing infrastructure investment plans (MEDC/DDA/WSU/PPP/DRP/RTA)
- Assess existing community conditions and asset inventory
- Prepare community requirements needed to meet minimum design standards
- Propose alternative development and conduct public outreach
- Provide environmental overview, implications, and public notification
- Provide Public Private Partnership financial feasibility
- Provide an EAC firm to supplement funding
- Prepare Design, Bid, and Build documentation
- Provide preferred EAC qualified construction contractors

NEIGHBORHOOD MASTER PLAN

After completing the city's infrastructure needs, analysis of its real estate market, determining schools and local public park locations, the EAC will help formulate the neighborhood marketplace.

- The Master Plan goals, objectives, milestones and deliverables will be published and widely communicated to all stakeholders.
- An EAC financial institution, along with other banking partners will accommodate small businesses with access to capital to draw from and help manage insurance, bonding, and material expenses as well as meet payroll requirements.
- The design and planning team will work with the city's zoning board to incorporate targeted community projects with other investors to enhance the overall community development program.
- The design and planning team will prepare a phasing plan to minimize disruption to residents and business community during demolition and construction.

While there are many different residential districts throughout the city, the basic neighborhood rezoning and configuration standard is based on a (3x3) three square mile area with the central (1x1) one square mile block containing the central marketplace and the Isuthu High School.

Also, the central square mile block contains a local public park, and multiple Isuthu Middle Schools. The outer (3x3) surrounding areas are made up of large green spaces, new housing developments and several Isuthu Elementary Schools.

Each community will have an opportunity to weigh-in to help shape the personality of the community features, characteristics, and supporting amenities.

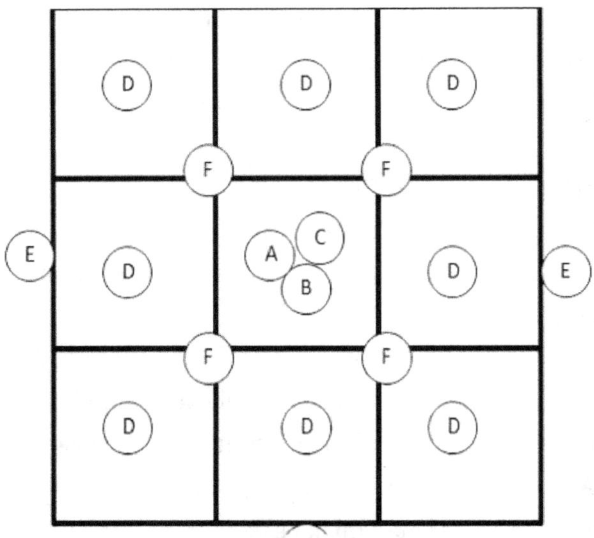

A – Central Isuthu Institute High School

B – Reginal Isuthu Institute Middle Schools

C – Mixed Use, Public Park, and Community Garden

D – Single Homes and Isuthu Institute (pk-5) Schools

E – No structures: tree-lined streets and bike lanes

F – Business Zones @ major intersections

F – Light Rail Connection

F – Bus Transit

CONSTRUCTION PROJECT MANAGEMENT

Upon adoption of the master plan, the community development moves into the project solicitation and construction phase under contract with a design-bid-build EAC architecture, engineering and construction firms.

- Because construction will be taking place concurrently all over the city, every project management team will include a relationship coordinator assigned to each community development to help manage disruption and address any environmental concerns, e.g., noise, dust, safety and impact on public transportation.
- Each community will have its own set of needs and financing individual projects depends on what is required to achieve the new zoning and configuration standards. Every project by community will have a design, bid, and build package prior to contract award.
- Each project will have a contractor and construction project assignment, defining scope of work, terms and conditions, unit cost and labor rates, as well as guaranteed margins. Because all projects will be managed through the enterprise's business integration management (BIM) system, there's no need to incentivize contractors to cut costs on quality.
- Each community will integrate a theme of connectivity through out the neighborhoods that will rival any city across America and around the world, complete with green spaces and monuments of great Black symbolism.

CITY OF DETROIT NEIGHBORHOODS

Neighborhood	Design Team	Contract Administrator	Project Team	Prime	Sub-Contractor	Tasks
Bagley	TBD	TBD	TBD	TBD	TBD	TBD
Barton-McFarland	TBD	TBD	TBD	TBD	TBD	TBD
Belmont	TBD	TBD	TBD	TBD	TBD	TBD
Berg-Lahser	TBD	TBD	TBD	TBD	TBD	TBD
Blackstone Park	TBD	TBD	TBD	TBD	TBD	TBD
Boynton	TBD	TBD	TBD	TBD	TBD	TBD
Briggs	TBD	TBD	TBD	TBD	TBD	TBD
Brightmoor	TBD	TBD	TBD	TBD	TBD	TBD
Carbon Works	TBD	TBD	TBD	TBD	TBD	TBD
Castle Rouge	TBD	TBD	TBD	TBD	TBD	TBD
Core City	TBD	TBD	TBD	TBD	TBD	TBD
Corktown	TBD	TBD	TBD	TBD	TBD	TBD
Delray	TBD	TBD	TBD	TBD	TBD	TBD
Eight Mile Wyoming	TBD	TBD	TBD	TBD	TBD	TBD
Eliza Howell	TBD	TBD	TBD	TBD	TBD	TBD
Fiskhorn	TBD	TBD	TBD	TBD	TBD	TBD
Fitzgerald	TBD	TBD	TBD	TBD	TBD	TBD
Five Points	TBD	TBD	TBD	TBD	TBD	TBD
Franklin Park	TBD	TBD	TBD	TBD	TBD	TBD
Grandale	TBD	TBD	TBD	TBD	TBD	TBD
Herman Gardens	TBD	TBD	TBD	TBD	TBD	TBD
Hubbard Richard	TBD	TBD	TBD	TBD	TBD	TBD
LaSalle Gardens	TBD	TBD	TBD	TBD	TBD	TBD
Littlefield	TBD	TBD	TBD	TBD	TBD	TBD
Mexicantown	TBD	TBD	TBD	TBD	TBD	TBD
Michigan-Martin	TBD	TBD	TBD	TBD	TBD	TBD
Millennium Village	TBD	TBD	TBD	TBD	TBD	TBD
Minock Park	TBD	TBD	TBD	TBD	TBD	TBD
North Corktown	TBD	TBD	TBD	TBD	TBD	TBD
NW Goldberg	TBD	TBD	TBD	TBD	TBD	TBD
Oakman Boulevard	TBD	TBD	TBD	TBD	TBD	TBD
Oakwood Heights	TBD	TBD	TBD	TBD	TBD	TBD
Old Redford	TBD	TBD	TBD	TBD	TBD	TBD
Parkland	TBD	TBD	TBD	TBD	TBD	TBD
Petosky-Otsego	TBD	TBD	TBD	TBD	TBD	TBD
Riverdale	TBD	TBD	TBD	TBD	TBD	TBD
Russell Woods	TBD	TBD	TBD	TBD	TBD	TBD
Springwells	TBD	TBD	TBD	TBD	TBD	TBD
The Eye	TBD	TBD	TBD	TBD	TBD	TBD
Westwood Park	TBD	TBD	TBD	TBD	TBD	TBD
Winship	TBD	TBD	TBD	TBD	TBD	TBD

THE CITY OF DETROIT PROPOSAL

The vision and role of the Basecamp is to convert the city of Detroit into the greenest city in the world amongst large metropolitan areas. The physical city has been pruned back like a rose bush, and now ready to grow brilliant new buds better than before! The city of Detroit Infrastructure Plan will create a new diversified economy, spawning new markets across the city and adjacent suburbs. The city's existing roadway system can move a million vehicles per hour. By utilizing smart applications, the city can maximize facilities to reduce pollution and enhance visitors' experience. The switch to autonomous electrical vehicles, Mobility as a Service (MaaS) will benefit new entrepreneurs greatly as the concept transforms people's traveling journey, which will include an expanded transportation network, connecting commuter and light rail and passenger drone crafts to transport individuals and packages across the region, including connecting them to commercial airports. Large tech companies and OEM manufacturers are already exploring and conducting research to redesign regional transit and major thoroughfares and corridors to connect with the city of Detroit. By reconstructing the city's infrastructure to support the vast mobility network will achieve an unparalleled economy of scale and a return on investment to the region.

Only large well-funded corporations have the resources to leverage Detroit's roads to accommodate new commuter and light rail and build on its freight lines and high concentration of land assets to manage supply chain more effectively and efficiently. New manufacturing processes and delivery methods will emerge along with appropriate product packaging. The development of automated manufacturing corridors that straddle along rail lines, road routes and designated drone delivery flight paths will change residential configuration. The city of Detroit demolition program is an opportunity to redesign the new city landscape by reclaiming blighted thoroughfares and boulevards and converting them into green spaces. The large number of vacant buildings in Detroit and the surrounding suburbs will be demolished, repurposed, and reimagined. There are many proposed applications for vacant buildings; from designing multi-purpose green buildings to facilitating urban farms to provide fresh fruits and vegetables. The city could leverage its large tracts of vacant land by leasing them to industrialists to construct renewable energy sites.

The city of Detroit proposal will serve as the next frontier of the experiential age; creating new workplaces that offer work-life balance is essential to repurposing the city's neighborhoods. Every citizen will play a role in the new economy; with large industrialist firms building infrastructure, mid-level corporate firms providing professional services to an influx of new small franchise business owners who will offer Customer Experience as a Service (CEaaS) to personalize goods and services in healthcare, financial services and wealth planning, healthy dining, diet and exercise to customize cosmetics, hair & nail care, including schooling, higher education to memorializing one's life will emerge in the new virtual world of experiential lifestyle.

REGIONAL MOBILITY & TRANSPORTATION PLANNING

The implementation of a mobility strategy and community planning will serve as a catalyst to alter the trajectory of economic conditions in the greater Detroit Area. First, let's examine the output of a mobility value proposition, beginning with a Southeastern Michigan Commuter T-Train Plan to facilitate the movement of people, product development siting and supply chain routes. Detroit could increase its regional marketability by investing in commuter rail service. A central point of interest is the connectivity to Detroit Metropolitan Airport. The Airport Authority must work in cooperation with inter-state government agencies to ensure they can link the high employment centers in Northwest Ohio and Southeastern Michigan via a fast train from Toledo to the airport.

A study completed by the city of Toledo promoted a T-Train concept (CSXT Toledo-Flint) line that would link the (MDOT Detroit-Ann Arbor) line creating the basis of robust passenger transit-oriented development. Michigan Department of Transportation (RTA) published a master plan for southeastern Michigan that combines commuter rail, light rail, and bus route connections. These plans will determine people's mobility and access to jobs, goods, and services. As part of Michigan Avenue Connected

Corridor (Autonomous Mobility) with the Detroit Region Aerotropolis (DRA), proposes a southern Wayne County S-line Light-Rail, like the Downtown Detroit's Q-line will drive international exposure to these emerging commerce centers (small-town retailers), parks, and neighborhoods to encourage a new residential tax base.

To reimagine the communities within the Detroit Aerotropolis Region will require an effective engagement strategy. The profile value curve illustrates the consensus needed from inter-governmental agencies across the region to attract new investors. The same methodology must be applied to the greater Detroit Metropolitan area to seek consensus from taxpayers to pass a mileage to fund commuter rail construction, determine the best routes and placement of electrical buses and shuttle depots, to urban farming and renewable energy sites. The pre-work will provide a roadmap to potential investors, suppliers, and manufacturers sites and eliminating permits and zoning barriers. Investors need to demonstrate how each community will benefit from specific business segments, i.e., transportation, logistics & warehousing, manufacturing, drone technology and green renewables. Like many metropolitan areas across the U.S., Detroit's infrastructure is nearing the end of its useful life expectancy and now needs to address it. According to the American Society of Engineers, there is a $177 billion estimated investment gap in electricity generation and delivery, and an $836 billion backlog of highway and bridge improvement needs.

The estimate for water is even higher, projected at ($1 trillion) needed for buried drinking water infrastructure. Henry Ford built an entire community around his automotive manufacturing facility along the Rouge River commonly known as the Ford River Rouge Complex (a.k.a., the Rouge Plant). Because of his vision for vertical integration to drive a continuous process necessitated the need to control all aspects of the manufacturing process, including the people who worked at the plant. Ford leveraged the railroads of Vanderbilt, and the steel from Andrew Carnegie, oil from John Rockefeller and financial backing from JP Morgan to transform the middle-class worker and the lifestyle of the average American well into the next century.

While it may seem daunting to think about the cost to rebuild America's crumbling infrastructure. With a focus on the city of Detroit makes the infrastructure task and cost more manageable. Utilizing private firms to construct utilities, bridges and roadways is nothing new to government agencies. The private sector is better equipped, organized, and disciplined to manage large-scale infrastructure projects more efficiently.

REGIONAL VALUE CHAIN PLANNING

The Mega-infrastructure investor-owners of the EAC conglomerate will create new corporations. Like the Industrialization Age of the 20th Century, the Digital Age (aka, Information Age) of the 21st Century will create new wealth and entrepreneurs who will find ways to continuously improve and reinvent the way humans live, play and work in what is being phrased as the Experiental Age. The EAC must be prepared to compete with domestic and international innovators seeking to provide new solutions and delaying others from penetrating into their market space. While it is important to keep jobs in-house, foreign investment is unavoidable, as access to capital is critical to the innovative process.

The rapid development of electronics will continuously drive MaaS, dictating how we design, produce, and distribute food, clothing, homes, and consumer goods real-time. Innovators will require creativity in time management, the ability to scale up and the capacity to deliver the goods faster. The need for skilled futurists, designers (landscape and city planners), computer scientists, architects, engineers, machinists, and supply chain modelers, as well as legal services and building contractors will be in high demand. These are not characteristics of a small business with little capital. To operate in this space, small boutique firms must collaborate with larger firms and establish solid partnerships to resemble large corporations with professional expertise necessary to acquire the necessary financial backing and meet procurement ordinance minimum standards.

The price of real estate and supporting sprawling infrastructure is not sustainable in the long-run and will necessitate the integration of warehouses and consolidated production facilities supported by regulated drone delivery channels in urban areas. Other infrastructures like vertical parking systems for autonomous battery-operated vehicles will need to be built next to where people work and connect to aerial drone passenger service. The establishment of high-density drone package delivery services will give way to passenger air transportation drone ports and drone highways in the sky.

There are companies already on the precipices of breakthrough strategies to unpack the manufacturing value chain, targeting solutions for industries, providing cost-effective functionality and capability for consumers, creating a safe environment to conduct business and making transactions an emotional experience. Companies like UPS, FedEx, DHL, and Amazon are already experimenting with last mile drone delivery concepts that will eventually become commonplace. While it is unlikely new cities can afford to construct an underground subway infrastructure system on the scale of New York City, it is certainly conceivable cities can establish a passenger drone service overhead. These drones will be autonomously connected to structures to transport people from the center city to medium and large-hub airports across the region.

The power of data management via the integration with the internet of things and cyber security will redefine the way humans interact with technology and with one another. An influence of our everyday lives will be dictated, in part, by population density, energy and mobility. Again, the advantages of corporate scale are to facilitate the adoption of communications (fiber) and micro-grids, and the investment of renewable energy sources adjacent to large cities, including the transition from petroleum-based service stations to battery-powered services.

Attracting people back to the city will require communities to make the shift and think about how to make densely populated areas more favorable. The communities of color should not be duped by the false narrative of a greener pasture in the suburbs. The idea of building an infrastructure like the city of Detroit, or other large cities abandoned during White flight again would be costly. Traditional gentrification models bear this out, as population shifts are already underway aimed at controlling central infrastructure utilities and city core assets. Access to healthy food choices is a simple issue to overcome by shifting food supply through community gardens, commercial urban farms, and green buildings will alleviate many ills of inner-city dwellers. Simply rethinking how to use natural resources represents a paradigm shift towards traditional agrarian approaches. By shifting African American diets will reduce high-blood pressure and diabetes. When the economy returns, home renovation and construction will experience tremendous growth. The opportunity to reclaim existing commercial space and repurpose idle office space by converting it into living assemblages will cater to the needs of emerging Experiential Age city dwellers.

Today, Arab Americans and others are buying up property in the City's depressed areas, which is a good thing. However, they are profiting at the expense of African Americans, while they create institutional wealth for their families, alter the course of local politics and promote their success stories. Please don't blame these outside groups directly, as they are being opportunistic by capitalizing on the weakness of less organized poor communities. African Americans have a huge opportunity. Regardless of your nationality, anyone with some insight and innovative thinking can lead the way when it comes to developing new electrical engines and components, solid state battery technology and production and developing new travel and mobility products tied to MaaS.

The question remains, who will develop these new markets? Why should the EAC wait around for someone else to develop them? Attracting talent to Detroit, especially African American engineers is crucial. Many engineers graduating from Michigan universities are choosing to leave the area in favor of the South, creating a talent gap. What good is it to have billions of dollars in infrastructure spending and nobody to employ from the region. If the EAS fails to harvest new talent from the Black community in the near-term, will result in another lost generation and set the reparation argument back another decade or indefinitely. Because the words on these papers are available for all to read, other people will be giving the roadmap and an opportunity to drive the agenda when it's up to African Americans to decide.

MAJOR NEIGHBORHOOD PLANNING

The city of Detroit value position is to revive the city landscape by leveraging Detroit's baroque design and reclaiming its thoroughfares, boulevards, and open spaces to spearhead economic development and reimagine a city that will improve the lives of all Detroiters. The proposal rests on the relationship between municipality and public-private partnerships to promote an inverse gentrification initiative aimed to attract high concentrations of people of color. Regardless of the neighborhood, the planning template calls for the integration of renewable technology, electrical vehicle charging stations, and other amenities, including within walking distance to a community marketplace.

There is no doubt that the development of parks and light rail integrated with tree-lined thoroughfares, boulevards and green open spaces will attract people, especially people of means to generate new investment and economic growth. Detroit could be the envy of the country for its new sophisticated urban hotspots. By re-imagining major avenues and converting them into inner-city green parkways where bicyclist can travel from one end of the city to connecting parks, giving way to different cultures and community marketplaces. The restoration value proposition is to incorporate a light rail line similar to M-1: Woodward Avenue (Q-line); East Jefferson Avenue (R-line), M-3: Gratiot Avenue (E-line), M-5: Grandriver Avenue (N-line), US12: Michigan Avenue (Z-line), and the Northland-Greenfield Avenue (G-line) that connects to the Grandriver Avenue (N-line).

Northland (Southfield, Michigan): While outside the city limits of Detroit, its location and land assets are significant. Southfield, Michigan has become a predominantly African American suburb and home to many national corporations. The Northland Shopping Mall was the largest shopping mall in the world when it opened on March 22, 1954. The Victor Gruen design was an open-air pedestrian mall with various structures surrounding a four-level J. L. Hudson department store. The mall closed on March 22, 2015.

Detroit's Outer Drive was originally designed as a pleasurable bypass (like a parkway) that encircled the entire city, as one can travel nearly 40 miles from one end of the city to the other connecting Chandler Park on the east side to a proposed renovation of Wayne County's public park jewel, River Rouge Park, as well as several suburbs on the west side. The revitalization and restoration value proposition calls for establishing West Outer Drive Parkway, eliminating on-street parking, and adding bicycle lanes.

The plan includes the Demolition of abandon structures and restoring green spaces, lighting, and erecting prominent African American Statues to enhance neighborhoods from Rosedale Park and Grandmont, Winship, Bagley, and Greenwich Park, ending at Livernois' Avenue of Fashion at the outskirts of the stately Palmer Woods neighborhood. East Outer Drive (State Fair) will be open to International Gentrification.

Detroit's Grand Boulevard is an adaptation to Baron Georges-Eugene Haussmann designs, who designed parks, broad streets, and a Grand Boulevard to make Paris, France beautiful. When Belle Islands was transferred from the State of Michigan to the city of Detroit, Mayor Hazen Pingree supported the idea and broke ground in 1891 to construct a ring road around the downtown area stretching 12 miles and three miles at its center point from the Detroit River. Because the Grand Boulevard split Woodward Avenue, established an East Grand Boulevard and West Grand Boulevard, both recognized as a major attraction to the city where sections had center islands decorated with trees, shrubbery, and flowerbeds. In the central section of Grand Boulevard, known as Midtown, is home to Henry Ford Hospital, the Fisher Theater, the Detroit Pistons Training Facility, and other businesses. The restoration value proposition focuses on the section where the Grand Blvd. connects Jeffereson Avnenue to Grandriver Avenue on the west side to Gratiot Avenue all the way around to Jefferson Avenue, on the east, ending at Belle Isle Park. The famous park was designed by renowned Landscape Architect, Frederick Law Olmsted during 1880s, more than twenty years after he designed New York's Central Park.

Detroit's Oakman Boulevard was named after master developer, Robert Oakman. Mr. Oakman purchased the tract of land in 1908. He convinced his friend, John Dodge to invest in the project to garner support from Ford Motor Company's, Henry Ford to help back the road construction that would connect Ford's Highland Park Plant to the Dearborn Ford Rouge Plant (originally proposed names were Ford Highway, then Oakman Highway, and finally Oakman Boulevard). Oakman's wife, Mamie Moross, was the daughter of Joseph Moross, builder of the Grand Boulevard. Mr. Oakman realized his boulevard name's sake was no match to the Grand Boulevard, with its upper-middle class homes and manicured islands. He decided to shift his master plan to Colonial Revival, English, and Tudor architecture. It is recorded that Mr. Oakman imported trees from around the world so future students could learn about botany. The value proposition calls for restoring homes and landscaping islands between Fullerton Avenue and Linwood Avenue. The reimagined thoroughfares, boulevards and parkways will anchor to Detroit's Estate Communities, serving as a catalyst for developing small community village-like atmospheres. The utmost goal is to create an environment for professional African Americans to migrate back to the city to transform neighborhoods.

ESTATE COMMUNITY PLANNING

The estate communities will serve as EAC corporate office centers to anchor community business zones:

Boston-Edison; formerly the Boston-Edison District held under various land grants (One grant held by the mayor of the city of Detroit, John R. Street, and three grants held by Senator, Thomas Palmer), until the Joy, Newberry and Voigt Families took control and begin developing the Voigt sub-division (Midtown). The sub-division consisted of 900 custom-designed estates situated on spacious lots. The sub-division was integrated into the city of Detroit in 1891.

Indian Village: developed by François Rivard and Jacque St. Aubin who were recipients of French land-grant ribbon farms. A long narrow strip of land gave farmers access to river frontage. Indian Village is an affluent neighborhood located on Detroit's east side. The homes were built by prominent architects during the early 20th Century. The prominent citizens included Edsel Ford and Henry Leland, founder of Lincoln and Cadillac luxury cars.

Palmer Woods: acquired by a developer named Charles Burton. Mr. Burton hired Ossim Simmonds to develop a master plan community with custom estates on curvy avenue. The land was originally owned by Senator Thomas Palmer (mentioned earlier). Mr. Thomas donated 188 acres south of Seven Mile Road to the city of Detroit, which today, is known as Palmer Park, north of Highland Park, MI. The land north of Seven Miles was passed to his descendants who sold the land to Charles Burton, the developer of Palmer Woods.

Rosedale Park: developed in the early 20th Century as a streetcar and automobile suburb, designed in Colonial Revival Brick and Tudor architecture covering 340 acres (Grandmont-Rosedale area). While less grand than the previous estate communities, it was still home to an elite group of professional residents.

INVERSE GENTRIFICATION PLANNING

The inverse gentrification model is the process of reimagining, renovating, and reinstating previous inhabitants to the district that conforms to modernized standards. Our value proposition is to raise income levels and attract a new crop of motivated residents from all racial and ethnic groups back to the city.

Estate Gentrification: under DIPA is designed to attract affluent people in the restoration of some of Detroit's finest historic estates. While this is the smallest gentrification model, they are the most influential. Their integration poses the greatest investment to successfully integrate an African American gentrification model in adjacent neighborhoods. These communities will seamlessly transition into African American gentrification neighborhoods where they share shops, gathering places and high-quality public schools and places of worship.

African American Gentrification: under DIPA is designed to attract Black professionals to Northwest and Southeast Detroit; historically anything west of Woodward Avenue is considered the West Side, east of Woodward Avenue is the East Side. The goal is to work with existing rehabilitation programs, via EOZ, EDD, and PPP within the city to facilitate opportunities to reclaim adjacent neighborhoods (depending on the neighborhood), 1) combine multiple demolished lots into a single lot, 2) innovative remodels of existing homes, and 3) restoration of existing high-quality homes. The African American gentrification will be high-end homes with sophisticated shops and gathering places that will serve as buffers surrounding estate properties.

Affordable Housing Gentrification: under DIPA is designed for first-time home buyers and low-wage earners, primarily made up of all metro Detroiters. These dwellings will not be arranged like "Section-eight housing projects" of old, but integrated city neighborhoods planned with a sense of place, dignity, and ownership. Instead of renting, people will build owner equity, allowing them access to credit and the ability to advance. These communities will be seamlessly transitioned into adjacent culturally diverse neighborhoods to share shops, gathering places, public schools, and places of worship.

Hispanic Gentrification: under DIPA focuses on expanding the Hispanic heritage and culture beyond Mexican town throughout SW Detroit. Latinos are significant contributors to Detroit's rich history. The expansion will fully embrace the various Spanish-speaking people, cultures, architecture, and commerce. The community will complement existing and new international immigrants to the city of Detroit.

Millennial Gentrification: under DDA and DEGC is traditionally known for being predominantly young white professionals. These are professionals from all racial make-up that falls into the hipster culture. This group value amenities like MaasS, recycling, green spaces to reclaimed buildings and restoring historical architecture. The millennial gentrification is concentrated around the University of Detroit, Wayne State University (Midtown), Downtown and neighborhoods adjacent to Grosse Pointe.

International Gentrification: under MEDC and DIPA is set aside for new immigrants to populate Detroit. A new crop of cultures are welcome to settle in Detroit, from well-educated middle-income families in the northeast, west and southwest to the ultra-rich along the east river. Also, to attract back other eastern Europeans to make Hamtramck and Highland Park home again.

Inverse Gentrification is all about doing things differently and creating the type of community's Black people really want and need. As result, new unchartered territories become available for creative minds to change the course of humanity. Gentrification is only a bad word if the people being displaced are on the losing end. If the EAC wants to control land use and how people share in the benefits, the old model of economic development no longer applies. This can only happen if you are at the table developing the policies and planning that goes into the materialization of true inclusion. Younger generations are entering the Experiential Age; and the EAC must ensure their engagement. The EAC must control the basic needs to sustain Black communities, and that is by recycling money through Black businesses. Reimaging the Black community and its marketplace is essential to the successful implementation of the Detroit proposal.

HUMAN INFRASTRUCTURE PLANNING

The DIPA will make way for small business owners to innovate at the granular level. The role of the foundation is to ensure people of color have access to opportunities that allow them to participate and benefit from the economic development process, while at the same time, attract new investors stemming from the regional mobility infrastructure. Human civilization always advances from one period to the next; regardless of the period, the EAC must provide those basic human psychological needs that will never change. Humans require food, shelter, and security. As human beings, we require a sense of love and belonging. We seek self-esteem, and ultimately, as we mature, we aspire to achieve self-actualization. Future entrepreneurs must determine what to produce, package, and how to deliver them, and not just for Black people, but for all people who want and need certain goods and services. It is the responsibility of the individual person to provide their own food, shelter, and security. While small businesses cannot build the mobility infrastructure or acquire large swaths of abandon buildings and convert them into green building and urban farms, the EAC would be well-positioned to fund start-ups and small manufacturing facilities near people living in these communities to produce the new products, as well as provide ways to deliver them. While some small businesses cannot build or renovate new homes or get into the Home Mortgages-Insurance game, the EAC must establish relationships with these new perspective home buyers to attract them to Detroit by selling and marketing a new lifestyle not available anywhere else. Similarly, for the financial services and financial planning segments, presents another opportunity for start-ups. Historically, under the guise of religious benevolence, European churches, UNICEF, and the United Nations have sought to guide African people on the continent. The same can be said for African Americans in the United States, as they continue to fall further and further behind on the global stage. Today, it is under the umbrella of progressive politics, academia and social justice that "woke" progressives create their version of social justice along with their hand-picked social activist. The University of Michigan (Law School and Business School) launched a new crop of outside innovators to shape small businesses in Detroit. Think about who is shaping the plan, doing the hiring, and providing the Job Training & Placement. These are opportunities for the EAC. It is important to leverage all the possible resources available, but the accountability rests with the people of the Black community. There was a time when healthcare was provided by a family doctor who had an office in the neighborhood. Because of medical malpractice lawsuits manufactured by the legal industrial complex, has all but eliminated independent physicians and small locally owned and managed clinics. The innovation of providing affordable healthcare with minimum risk is another opportunity for the EAC. The problem with healthcare, in part, is due to artificial barriers that prevent new entrants from participating, and left to large hospital systems to control market share. The solution is two-fold, one, find a way to improve dietary health, and two, develop a system that integrates personal health records, mobilizes medical equipment, and delivers alternative medical treatment and prescriptions cheaper and faster. One huge opportunity for African Americans centers around food and food sources. African Americans suffers from hypertension and heart disease at an alarming rate. Obesity, poor diet, and lack of exercise contribute greatly to these diseases amongst Black people. Black people must be willing to change their eating habits by consuming appropriate portions of multigrain, seasonal fruits and vegetables daily. This is not possible for poor Black communities. But by controlling urban farms will enable African Americans to make healthy choices and lengthen life expectancy. The large lobbyists groups will be out in full force to influence regulations and legislation to reject any form of market disruption. The power of love and belonging is transcendental and a vital part of the human experience. Most people are connected by their religion, as such; spirituality can never be outsourced or commoditized. COVID-19 has changed the dynamic of being in a confined space but has not changed the need to be close to one another. Take African American places of worship, as many are disconnected from those in need. The challenge facing congregations is a lack of ownership and power over the community's wealth where their flock lives and this dysfunction of the Black church and its flock is problematic. Black churches must learn new ways to reach people considering the COVID-19 pandemic. The sustainability of the church cannot survive if the church building is located outside the community it serves. The church building must be a beckon of hope within the community it serves, so even if the people cannot fellowship inside the building, they can see no value of maintaining the building itself. Even the sustainability of social media, e.g., Facebook will soon come to an end, as social media fragments into smaller platforms. The sense of belonging will continually evolve in a less productive manner as we have seen with the fractioning of political discourse only reinforces the need for an innovative narrative to restore leadership and order in the Black community – a community with no physical boundaries. The vanity part of human beings is the need of self-awareness of one's sense of importance. Possessing beautiful things and luxuries dates back centuries well into ancient times. It depicts success and accomplishment. The Detroit market will facilitate a home construction boom.

The mobility corridors will provide a group of HGTV *Detroit Styles* live-in neighborhood planners (e.g., Bargain Block) to market and design home renovation projects, expanding on Detroit Month of Design. It is no secret that small business owners and local artisans make up the largest group of employers in the country. They will find a way to serve the needs of their community. If the people of that community cannot provide it, then others will come along to fill the niche. Each neighborhood will include traditional small shops like tattoo parlors, hair, and nail and massage salons. But, with the advent of new home buyers, a new crop of artisans (plumbers, tile, millwork, glass makers, landscape designers, and interior decorators) will emerge to cash in on the new growth. The need for innovation studios will emerge to attract new education platforms and research & development start-ups. People will want to be seen in new public squares and associated with certain neighborhoods, advancing even more public works to attract international investments and immigrants to the city. The coronavirus made its presence known during births, weddings, and deaths. It is important as a society that we learn how to celebrate new life, special events and the last stages of life without interruption. From cradle to grave, innovation can ensure connectivity, emotional support, and admiration, as well as provide people with dignity in their final days. Amassing large sums of capital is where we transfer big ideas to reality. The EAC must take best practices from the financial services market and identify opportunities to continuously improve upon it to generate value, not only to African Americans, but to all venture capitalist and industrialist around the world. The value chain of the city of Detroit is the largest city in the State of Michigan, and it has the largest concentration of fresh water in the nation, including an abundant of agrarian land suitable for diverse types of crops. The city of Detroit can leverage its proximity to the fresh water supply and solid infrastructure (albeit, at the end of its useful life) to support the next generation of supply chain, manufacturing, mobilization, and communications, strategically positioned in the Midwest region of the country. Despite the seasonal weather in southeastern Michigan, the new social and economic climate will attract intelligent people and entrepreneurs from all over the world to take part in this new idea of enlighten African Americans, taking the lead to forge a new crop of wealthy residence and anyone else who choose to invest in the new emerging economy resulting from African American reparations. The first step towards African American reparation is outlined in the call-to-action agenda prepared by the author in the final essay. If Black people do not come together, it will be difficult and continuously weaken efforts to innovate markets and create a world designed around common morals and values. The most powerful ways to transform Black people is to connect with a purpose. It is important to accomplish everything presented in this paper to grow wealth and pass it on to the next generation. Once political favor is achieved, the foundation and the enterprise must help the less fortunate and create opportunities for others still left behind and tell his-story or her-story for future generations. The legacy of Detroit's past was defined by racial segregation and discrimination as Black people migrated from the South. While they were not welcomed, Black people must welcome others and treat new residents with kindness and openness. It comes back to living with a purpose. Frederick Douglas recorded in his memoirs that he lost his drive for social consciousness after the Emancipation because he thought his mission was done, but he recognized he was wrong. The movement had just begun. The purpose of Black people in America is not limited to reparations – it's just the be beginning! Up until now, African Americans have been preparing to lead, and to become accountable to their family, people, and country. The call to action is not a slogan for Black people. It is a request for all Americans to continue our efforts to make America a more perfect union.

REPARATIONS DELIVERABLES

AFRICAN AMERICAN INFRASTRUCTURE ROADMAP

- **THE AFRICAN AMERICAN REPARATIONS ACT OF 2030**
  - AFRICAN AMERICAN INFRASTRUCTURE BILL
    - LEGISLATIVE LANGUAGE
    - PASSAGE BY CONGRESS
  - CODE OF FEDERAL REGULATION LANGUAGE
    - ENGINEERING STANDARDS
    - CERTIFICATION STANDARDS
    - INDUSTRY COMPLIANCE REQUIREMENTS
    - MATERIAL HANDLING REQUIREMENTS
    - APPRENTICE CERTIFICATION BODIES
- **THE CITY OF DETROIT INFRASTRUCTURE PLAN (NATIONAL TEMPLATE)**
  - DETROIT INFRASTRUCTURE PLAN AUTHORITY (DIPA) ORDINANCE
    - WATER & SANITARY
    - ROADS, BRIDGES & TUNNELS
    - UNDERGROUND UTILITIES
    - COMMUNITY DEVELOPMENT & PLANNING
      - FINANCIAL SERVICES
      - CONSTRUCTION & MANAGEMENT
      - HOUSING , PARKS & URBAN FARMING
      - EDUCATION: (PK-5) to 12 ISUTHU INSTITUTES
      - INTERDENOMINATIONAL FAITH COUNCIL
      - JOB SECTORS RECRUITMENT & PLACEMENT

THE CONVERSATION

The call to action is not only for African Americans but all Americans are welcome to help shift our country's mindset. However, Black leaders must take the lead to transform their condition and the consciousness of their people. The consciousness of Black people has been in a state of inertia predicated on destructive and distorted truths. History has shown us that to change the course of a people's liberation often requires a divine intervention revealed to us in the physical world through material things. The role African Americans played in shaping the United States and their impact on the world were highlighted throughout the previous papers, from influencing science and medicine, politics and legislation to sports and entertainment. Despite the long delay descending from the people of the Atlantic Slave Trade, it appears they are now ready to ascend to their rightful place as head of its own table prepared to make decisions that affect its own destiny.

African Americans are amongst the most diverse groups in the U.S. A significant domination descended from sub-Saharan enslaved Africans. Research shows thirty-five percent of Black men descent from a White male ancestry, resulting from a mulatto child during the slave era. Today, about nineteen percent of Black people have twenty-five percent European ancestry. One percent of African Americans have fifty percent European ancestry.

To evoke the profound sentiments of author and activist, James Baldwin, who said what is to become of the American Negro "*N*gg*r*" invented by America? An inference of African American inferiority expanded beyond slavery and morphed into an affectionate and acceptable term used in certain quarters of the black population. How long will America need them around? Is this the time when we closed the period of these former enslaved and beleaguered Black people? Is this the time when America allows all its people to achieve their full potential without interference?

If America truly wants to heal and move forward with reparations, certain hard truths must occur, and it's not about shaming the American people or seeking handouts from the government or embracing an extreme canceled culture. It's about having an open and honest conversation about how to move the country forward.

THE CONVERSATION

- PREFACE
- INTRODUCTION
- THE PREPARATION OF PURPOSE
- A CALL TO ACTION

PREFACE

These final words summarize my appeal to encourage an American ideology to heal the country through reconciliation. I want to finish my thoughts with candor, as the Manifesto of Emerging American Capitalist (MEAC) ends. I hope that my writing will not be in vain and that someone will see the value of moving the conversation forward for the collective understanding and to help resolve the divisions amongst the American people to achieve African Americans reparations. For my entire life, all I thought about was achieving the American dream. Despite my humble beginnings, I always believed that someday, my life would get better, and it did ultimately! Also, I thought during my lifetime, that the Rev. Dr. Martin Luther King, Jr. "I have a dream" speech would come true too. As a young boy, I was not aware of the complexity of complexion and what it meant to be Black until I experienced it first-hand. I have seen people, places, and things I can never stop thinking or knowing about, which is the basis of my purpose and preparation. My educational progression from grade school through high school did little to prepare me for how to deal with discrimination and racism, as it only personified the victimization of a helplessness mindset. I was blessed to attend college right out of high school where I learned about the real atrocities against African Americans. I know a big part of my confusion and internal conflicts with social injustice, economic inequities and cultural identity stemmed from my paternal Mulatto ancestry. All was revealed growing up amid the Black revolutionary movement. As I grew older, there were many occasions where I checked out of the conversation and stood on the sidelines. I witnessed the polarized dialogue amongst Black people, and conversely, listen to the tense debate about interracial relationships between Blacks and Whites spiral out of control. Everyone seems to be talking passed one another without building consensus or trying to understand what we need to do to achieve our goals together? I can understand if you think the ideas presented in this essay are on one hand simplistic or on the other, overwhelming. The stratification of Black people is complex with varying external forces at play, and many different opinions to consider. That's why I want to start small and grow organically.

Imagine with me, if you will, dropping a pebble in the middle of a smooth pond, the pebble creates a ripple effect from where the stone entered the water. Those ripples grow and expand further as they travel from the center, and that's the intent of the MEAC. To implement an African American reconciliation that coalesces all the other positive initiatives, bringing them along to facilitate social change and inclusiveness. It is not productive to capitulate to the centuries of intra-Black fighting as to which approach is best since the overarching goal is to achieve social-economic balance for Americans as a whole. If there is to be a category of African Americans in the future, Black people must come together to make sure it happens. This is not the time to be afraid of failure or false narratives of defeatism.

It might be messy and awkward at first, but eventually Black people will overcome their shortcomings. African Americans already proved they can achieve anything! Yes, African Americans were tortured, imprisoned, and deprived, exploited, and discriminated against to the point of ignorance and dysfunction. But despite everything done to them as a people, they have persevered to become inventors, scientist, researchers, engineers, and planners who can plan and oversee strategic military operations, manage large cities and mega-hub commercial airports, leaders and captains of industries, great constitutional legal minds, educators, legislators, and even become The President of the United States of America! If I played poker, one would conclude that I would not be very good because I wear my emotions like an open book. I am, by myself, nothing. I came from poverty but compelled to keep writing. There are many parallels in history I can draw from about the journey of enslaved people who arose from bondage to find their way to the promised land. It pains me to listen to other people, saying it's impossible for Black people to unite after decades of being divided and shattered from colonialism and slavery. How I see it in my mind's eye, spirit, and soul won't allow me to accept these opinions. I heard from an old wise man back in the day who use to say that Black people were asleep. The masses need not talk about the excuses to right the wrongs, but simply move forward by doing the difficult things. It is wonderful that a few Black people succeeded in garnering great wealth, prestige and influence or by whatever measure labeled success by society. The goal of this paper is to provide context for getting everyone on the same page when it comes to African American reparations. It is my hope that Black people will not senselessly wait around for the U.S. government or progressive legislators to craft, yet another failed version of social reform to satisfy their sensibility. I hope you choose to participate in the conversation to facilitate healing of the country we all love and cherish.

INTRODUCTION

I believe it's time for a conversation about African American reparations. I believe if it doesn't happen now, it may never be another opportunity to get it done in my lifetime. The constant struggle of racial injustice, White indifference, and bias political debate will never heal America's wounds. Only forgiveness and acceptance will endure. My concerns for America are genuine; not only am I an American but, an American who understands our problems. My intent is not to shame the American people in supporting the MEAC. I only hope by sharing my convictions it will resonate with you and bring about a common understanding. I understand that my time on this earth is finite and grows near every day, as I have wasted so much of my precious time as a young person consumed with chasing false dreams and images. Please note I do not have any regrets, as with age comes wisdom and I believe this was the plan for me.

I truly believe my experiences have shaped me and gave me purpose. I have nothing to prove because my motives are not about getting rich to feed my ego or impress others, but more so to live up to my responsibilities by improving the lives of other people. My motivation for writing the MEAC is about sharing ideas, and hopefully it will give way to a better America. I believe African Americans will overcome their scars of bondage and achieve greatness with forgiveness and humility. It is amazing how the British were able to compel people of other ethnicities (e.g., India, China, and Africa) to succumb to their colonialist model and come to accept their standards of beauty and norms over their own cultural value system. It is my hope that we will no longer care about skin color, hair texture and European features, but to define our own forms of beauty, style, and imagery.

The MEAC never intended to tackle implications of religion, political affiliation, and sexual orientation, as these issues are not limited to any single race or ethnic group. We either accept these differences or fall backwards in the ethos of human evolution. If these are going to serve as roadblocks that prevent Black people from engaging one another in a meaningful and transformational manner, then I believe you missed the point of this book. I love all people and cultures, no matter where they come from, as all lives matter, but I am bound to improving the lives of African Americans since they are the ones in peril.

According to my genetic markers, I am (forty-seven percent) Irish from my father's ancestry, (thirty-five percent) Nigerian from my mother's ancestry and (eighteen percent) other ethnicities between them. The racial construct labeled me black because of my skin color. And therefore, being Black, it matters to me. As a person of color, I want Black people to be strong and respected by the rest of the nation and the world.

I believe in the ideas of the United States of America. It is not a White idea, but a transcendental concept that provides a place for all people to pursue their hopes and dreams. I must admit I am not fond of the slogan "I am unapologetically Black" because I think it's unnecessary. It only reinforces isolationism and a posture of defense. I am unapologetically, an American who happens to be Black and proud of it! The only thing standing in our way is our thinking, and that is something we can change. I have been blessed, and I have found with my blessing brought much criticism, jealousy, and envy from others. In the beginning, I would be disturbed by those who opposed me, those who rejected me and tried to pull me down. Over time, I learned that I cannot allow negative people to steal my joy or distract me from my purpose.

After all the information presented thus far, please allow me to paint a simple picture in your mind's eye of how I envisioned we set the conversation in motion. First, I want to give the reader an opportunity to get to know a little about me personally. I believe I have been prepared to be honest, pure of heart, unselfish and loving. I want the reader to get to know me and how growing up in America shaped my point of view.

I believe time is running out for African Americans to establish a long-lasting and impactful legacy in the United States where the entire country will come to know and admire. It is not enough for a few Black people who sold their souls to represent what success looks like, while the larger population of African Americans continues to languish behind and who may never achieve the American dream. Most Black populations in the U.S. continue to live in crime-ridden neighborhoods with poor educational institutions and limited economic development where all the potential wealth passes through its neighborhoods while their local elected officials representing them are bound to outside financiers' and influencers; and this must change.

My viewpoint is less prophecy and poetry unlike the all inspiring orator, Dr. Martin Luther King, Jr. My thoughts evolved based on pragmatism, realism, and lots of optimism, but some may simply say idealism. I believe none of the concepts expressed in my writings are out of reach and would argue most are attainable within a decade from now if the American people are willing to put in the work. I want to say upfront; it was because of the hard work and commitment and personal sacrifices of many American freedom fighters that made my life possible and for that I am grateful. Because the job isn't done, I have an obligation to do my part to advance African American reparations.

"Identity is core and unavoidable part of all our lives – Our actions shape our identity, and in turn, our identity shapes our actions. Trying to pretend identity doesn't matter may make you feel better about yourself how others see you, and how their perceptions shape their actions" – Unknown 4/13/2013

THE PREPARATION OF PURPOSE

Please do not attempt to box me into a particular political bloc. Your opinion would be misplaced, as most consider me an enigma. At some point in everyone's life, they might question their existence and purpose on this earth. I like to think of myself as a person of science who believes in natural law. However, I came to believe in the supernatural, as I bear witness there is a higher power that I cannot explain by science and choose to call God. I am not a religious zealot, nor do I consider myself a religious person, as anyone who knows me knows I sometime use colorful language. I like to believe I am spiritually minded, unbounded by any institutionalized religious theology. The God of my understanding is incomprehensible to the human mind; everything learned and unlearned within and beyond the universe. From my perspective, human beings draw reasoning about what is real from a combination of scientific experimentation and interpretations, and then translated into languages, culture and norms by which people accept as truth. Therefore, everything that was written in the past was written to teach us and provide discernment, so that the endurance of knowledge can be taught to future generations, that we might find understanding and decide what is real.

I accept that no matter what I say about my life's journey and how I arrived at my beliefs, people will criticize me and attempt to define me by some social construct originating from where they come from or the specific period they lived. As the author, I wanted to keep my personal ideology out of the way to avoid placing perceived bias on you, the reader. I can confidently say, I had nothing to do with my parents. I did not choose them. But because of them, I was defined at birth. I would be labeled and assigned a value according to society. The label apportioned me a certain social hierarchy with limited access to opportunities and privilege. The labyrinth of life presented me with many hurdles and, in some cases, impenetrable barriers. Some people might say the challenge of my life was a disadvantage, but I came to believe they were the building blocks of my mental fortitude and spiritual gratitude. The culmination produced a life of contradictions;

I lived in poverty, yet I was surrounded by wealth. I was abandoned and neglected as a child, yet I was blessed to have many people come to love me and think of me as family. Despite being surrounded by ignorance, I received a world-class education.

I wish I could take credit for my accomplishments and survival. It is only through the kindness of others (by the grace of God) sent to watch over me, protect me, and keep me safe until I grew up. These kind people span across a lifetime from my youth through my professional career, enabling me to be open-minded towards other people and cultures. I learned that people are the same all over the world. During my travels I have seen the remnant of early fallen empires and believe if America doesn't change it will repeat the same failures. Why listen to me? I want to say something to my fellow Americans who love this country, and because I believe we can do better. While I may have been poor and experienced hopelessness, I have never considered myself a victim and nor should you! And now, I want to have an honest conversation with the American people to help heal our country before it's too late.

BIOGRAPHY SYNOPSIS

I was born, Bryant Wilfred Holt, on November 21, 1959, in Wayne, Michigan, next to the small working-class town where I lived, called Inkster, Michigan. My father, Vance Edwin Holt, served in the U.S Army during the Korean War. When he returned from the armed services, he worked for Fisher Body in Detroit. By the time I arrived, he was employed by the family business, a full-service Texaco Station, where he worked as a mechanic. My mother, La Don Jewel Woods, was an exceptionally neat homemaker. Prior to my birth, my parents already had five children: Bruce Edwin, Reiven Marshall, Dennis Wesley, Vanessa Dale, and Vance Carlton. The oldest, Bruce Edwin, was raised by my father's parents, John G. Holt, Senior and his wife, Julia S. Haley. The third child, Dennis Wesley, was raised by my father's mother's brother, Connie Lee Haley and his wife, Thelma Smith (a.k.a., Aunt Bay). My second oldest brother, Reiven, my sister Vanessa, and brother, Vance Carleton, and I lived with my parents. Both of my parents came from large families, so I have lots of cousins. My mother had four more children; Gary, Fabian, Anthony and Shawn by different fathers. Both of my father parents were descendants of interracial Irish parents (mulattos), as most people assumed they were Caucasian due to their skin color, hair texture and facial features.

Who influenced me? While I had lots of men in my life that shaped my professional and business acumen, it was the constant presence of women in my life whom I credit for my success. I don't want to discount the importance of having a father in a young boy's life, but I reject the notion that it is a pre-requisite to becoming a man. I have had nothing but strong determined woman in my life that guided me and held me accountable for my actions. At age eight, I was placed in the foster care of Ms. Lee Nell White, who was raising two of her own grandchildren who were the same age as me. We lived in southwest Detroit, surrounded by oil refineries and manufacturing facilities, bordering the city of River Rouge, Ecorse and Lincoln Park, Michigan. The factories produced lots of air pollution and we eventually moved to northwest Detroit, to the beautiful Winship neighborhood in the 48235-zip code. I eventually came to call Ms. White, Mama. Ms. White would not allow me to visit my biology family members unless it was under the supervision of social services. Ms. White taught me how to plant trees and vegetables and how to handle a rifle at age 12. She called me her little man. I was responsible for mowing the yard with a non-motorized push mower and doing the laundry with an old-fashioned washing machine that had a mechanical clothes ringer on the side. At times, she did not have a working vacuum, so I had to sweep the carpet with a straw broom. I never allowed my friends into my house because I was ashamed of Ms. White's housekeeping standards. I always held a job, starting out as a paper boy with the Detroit Free Press to working odd jobs as a handy man. I attended my freshman and sophomore year at Detroit's Cooley High School, where I served in the Reserve Officer Training Corp (ROTC) rising to the rank of Master Sargent and Drill Team leader. I completed required courses like pre-Algebra, American History, Literature and Swimming. Even though I never joined any gangs (e.g., Black Killers or Young Boys Incorporated), but by age 15, I became very rebellious during the summer of

1975 because I was restless and unchallenged. My Uncle Jerry and Aunt Evelyn (my father's sister) retrieved me from the Juvenile Delinquency center and enrolled me in Inkster High School for my junior year, where I made honor roll easily. Living with my biological family revealed many family issues unbeknown to me. The indiscretions of my parents and older siblings resurfaced in the most vicious and unsavory way. I responded poorly and embarrassed my Uncle Jerry, who taught at Inkster High School. As a result, he asked me to move out of his house at the end of that school year. One of my childhood friends (Narvin Davis) had me to ask his parents if I could stay at their home. It was Narvin's mother, Mildred Davis, a homemaker, who made me an offer I could not refuse. She agreed to let me live with them under two conditions; one, I stay in school and two; I get a job to help support myself. Ms. Davis would go on to feed me and wash my clothing as if I was her child. When I questioned my ability to survive, her motherly talks always reassured me that I was going to be fine. At the time of my high school graduation, all the relevant woman-folk who help raised me attended my graduation (Ms. White, Aunt Evelyn, and Ms. Davis). Also, an astounding thing happened, as I was surprised to see my biological mother, La Don in attendance. I graduated at age seventeen as class secretary, from Detroit's Redford High School during the summer of 1977. After the graduation ceremony, La Don asked me what I was planning to do after graduation. I told her that my buddies and I agreed to join the Navy. She declared you are not going to the military! *"Bryant, you're smart and I think you should go to college."* I stared at her as if she had two heads. I grew suspicious at this point because we never had a real relationship. I replied how do you expect me to pay for college? I can help you get the money and she proceeded to lay out the process and asked me to meet her downtown at the Veterans Administration (VA) Building and Social Security Office to complete the paperwork. I thought about it and made the following statement that I will never forget. *"I'll meet you downtown, but if you show up drunk, I am going to keep walking and never look back."*

Well, she showed up sober and secured me a regular monthly allowance from the VA and Social Security, provided I enroll in college as a full-time student. The agencies directed me to apply for the Federal Pell Grant and two years later I graduated from Wayne County Community College with an Associate of Science degree. I met my high school sweetheart, Shari Lynn Beasley, who was a junior at Redford High School the year I graduated. She would eventually become my wife. The main reason I fell in love with Shari was the easy way we communicated with each other. Shari's parents divorced when she was very young and I could sense how that impacted her. I understood what she wanted out of life, and I wanted the same things. She was reluctant to place trust in a man since her upbringing centered on the untrustworthiness of men associated with her mother's two failed marriages. As a young teenager, she felt there was more to me than my bad-boy persona. She has always latched on to my vision of the future and what could be and encouraged me to reach for the stars instead of settling for what's right in front of you. We were married on July 21, 1981, and my life became the most stable it has ever been. But at the same time, Shari endured the most turbulent and challenging phases of my life, providing unyielding support during my recovery of alcoholism – over 20 years sober. We purchased and restored the home that I grew up in from Ms. White. Both of our sons were delivered at Henry Ford Hospital main campus on West Grand Boulevard. I was considered a loving husband, good father, and responsible productive member of the community. I worked hard to earn her mother's respect. Her mother came to accept me as her son-in-law, because she realized I wasn't going anywhere. She discussed serious matters with me, things like how to invest my money, how to raise the children and treat my wife. She was not only my wife's mother, but she was my mother too. I watched how she made sacrifices to raise Shari and return to school to get her degree. I came to love and admire her for seeing things through to the end. Even though she wasn't wealthy, someone who didn't know her would assume she was well-off by the way she carried herself and presented herself. She loved fashion, often sewing her own clothes to supplement her wardrobe. She was a great cook and kept a beautiful home with nice furnishings. I learned how to maintain my property and enrich the lives of my family from Sharon Beasley. Shari and I gave unforgettable parties at our home. I was hired by E.I. de Nemours du Pont Corporation right out of Junior college, working my way up the ranks as I continued my education via the company's tuition reimbursement plan. The company relocated me from Troy, MI to Philadelphia, PA, to help design and build a new laboratory extension modeled after the Troy R&D Laboratory prototype. My wife and I were given access to the corporate jet to fly back and forth between Detroit and Philadelphia to find our new home. It was an exciting time for my family, as we resettled in Newark, DE. And while I had many great supervisors and bad ones, it wasn't until the alignment of an all-White women leadership team that gave me an opportunity of lifetime. I worked in DuPont's Performance Coatings division, strategic planning responsible for contributing $5 billion to the corporations' portfolio. It would be women who believed in my abilities and trusted me to execute the strategic business plan on a global scale. The Business Director of DuPont Performance Coatings was Rosanne Graham; the Director of Research & Development was Carol Senkler; and my direct supervisor, Research & Development Manager was Brenda Gelinas. Under their leadership, I was deployed to the Asia Pacific region (China, Taiwan, Thailand, Japan, and South Korea) as a Global Product Support Manager to leverage U.S. technology capabilities to Asia Automaker Original Equipment Manufacturers (OEM). Upon my return to the United States, I was promoted to Strategic Planning Manager and transferred to the World Headquarters in Wilmington, DE.

It's important for the reader to understand my perspective of women, even in western culture, represents the objective consciousness of our nation and maturity of its people.

Where have I been and what have I done? The places I have been, the things I have seen, and people I have encountered throughout my collegiate and professional career provided a window to the world that I might not have experienced if I lived in the same place and amongst the same people for my entire life. During my lifetime, I experienced lavish wealth to extreme poverty. I appreciated the diversity of thought as well as the different perspectives they offered regardless if I really understood them. I know that everything I was taught to believe proven not to be all together truthful during my adolescence. I attended Wayne County Community College, Wayne State University, and transferred to Olivet Nazarene University to earn a Bachelor of Business Administration, and later, repackaged my career after attending Columbia University in New York City for my Master of Science degree. Throughout my life I have participated in politics and social activism. Like most young college students, I participated in the social justice issues of the times, and in my case, the Post-Pan African movement of the 1980's. I served as the Local Conference Coordinator for Black Nation Day Conference, held at Wayne State University Center Building and the Hartford Memorial Baptist Church, in Detroit, Michigan. The keynote speaker was Minister Louis Farrakhan. I attended another less public conference in Atlanta, GA, where I came to my own conclusion about the fragility and irrationality of the Black separatist movements. As the only capitalist (and closet Republican at the time), I was scorned by some extreme radicals when I shared my early ideas of the Manifesto of Emerging American Capitalism (MEAC). I know firsthand the shortcomings of the separatist ideology; no capital, no political influence, and no compelling narrative to engage other people. I became a community organizer in northwest Detroit during the 80's when my children were very young. I coordinated efforts to spruce up our local parks. I spearheaded an initiative for block clubs to enhance the neighborhood. I worked with a local hospital to distribute food to senior citizens living in the surrounding communities. My job relocated me to Newark, Delaware, where I became the Civic Association President of Frenchtown Woods Development in the 90's. I assumed responsibilities from the builder to maintain community services; collect dues, oversee wetlands, maintain common-use open spaces, and contract snow and trash removal, as well as organize community events. During my time in the New York-New Jersey area, I was elected to the public office where I served as the downtown ward in Jersey City, NJ. Also, I was appointed by the mayor to serve on the environmental commission to oversee brownfield developments in the city. I had no limitations interacting with people from different cultures and religious backgrounds, as I enjoyed having a diverse group of people in my inner circle, from India, the Middle East, China, South America, and Africa. Over time, I developed the confidence to interact with anyone and take on any challenge. If I was not prepared to take on the challenge, I most certainly had the willingness to learn. A common theme throughout my life is I always start off at the bottom and work my way up to the top. My first real job out of college was with the DuPont Corporation, headquartered in Wilmington, DE, where I would spend the next 25 years holding various positions in research & development, manufacturing, and technical sales. I started out as a laboratory technician, and before I left the company, my major accomplishments included the design and construction of two laboratories; the first facility was in Philadelphia, PA at DuPont's Marshall R&D Laboratory and the second facility was at DuPont's Tio2 Manufacturing plant in Taipei City, Taiwan. I managed more than 40 highly educated laboratory technicians responsible for robotic paint application that simulated the manufacturing process for the big-three domestic OEM Automakers and Heavy-Duty Truck manufacturers like Freightliner, PACCAR, and Volvo Truck. As a Six Sigma black belt, I authored research studies and managed hundreds of laboratory test methods and standard operating procedures as part of the company's ISO-9000 certification program. Eventually, the company leveraged my technical and business acumen, as I was assigned projects that involved travels throughout North America, Europe, Asia Pacific, and South America to support DuPont coating products.

I finished my career as a strategic planning manager, responsible for deploying mature products in emerging markets. I credit DuPont for my business acumen and setting the standards of professionalism, discipline, and high performance – A truly great company! Prior to the divestiture of DuPont's Performance Coatings division to the Carlyle Group, I separated from DuPont to work for the Sears Holdings Corporation (SHC) for six years. Just like I started at DuPont, I had to prove myself. I was assigned a special project manager position, reporting directly to the general manager at the largest warehouse in the company's logistics network, located in Morrisville, PA. The warehouse yield throughput was grossly underperforming in carton per hour processing and order fulfillment accuracy. I leveraged much of my Six Sigma training from DuPont to improve output. I re-engineered the entire system from inbound freight process, analyzed the

Siemens conveyor processors and individual induction belts to outbound ordering software to maximize warehouse designed throughput to 6500 cartons per hour. In less than a year on the job, I was recruited by the vice president of logistics and relocated to the company headquarters in Hoffman Estates, IL. I was assigned the task of optimizing how products flowed through the company's entire supply chain network. Again, relying on my quality training, I developed an activity-based costing tool to drive flow path determination throughout the $1 billion supply chain network, in addition to determining potential risk factors associated with the implementation of the company's new web-based fulfillment platform. Before I elected to leave SHC, the executive vice president of logistics utilized my talent to help roll out the SHC portfolio project management to its 5000 world headquarters staff. I moved to the east coast, where I established an executive consultant firm, called Earth Innovations, LLC, briefly operating out of the New York and New Jersey area soon after graduate school. As the principal consultant, I provided 3D building models and cost analysis to prime contractors. I also work through a consultant agency assigned to AVON World Headquarter, New York, NY, where I was hired to oversee project management of new product development with a $177 million budget: containing over 100 products across multiple categories. I supported supply chain planning and coordination with manufacturing and marketing. I was recruited by the Office of the CEO at PR Newswire World Headquarters, New York, NY, responsible for growing revenue by seventeen percent. I managed P&L performance of a $30 million budget and reduced revenue leakage at their MultiVu media division. I was able to uncover $1.6 million in annual revenue loss due to non-collection of critical products and services. I changed jobs to care for my mother-in-law, Sharon, who was diagnosed with dementia. I again had to prove myself, by starting at the bottom as a consultant supporting information technology for airport executives. I was hired by a large hub commercial airport in the Midwest in 2015 where my talents were quickly recognized, as I was promoted every year. First, as the deputy director of planning, I oversaw the airport Master Plan, then director of strategy management, where I developed the modernization plan for a national reliever airport. I was eventually promoted to vice president of planning design & construction, where I changed the approach to capital improvement planning and capital project management. I was later appointed chief development officer, responsible for developing and managing the $590 million capital budget and strategic business plan for the airport system; that included the management of airport infrastructure, environment & sustainability, business development and real estate.

It's important for the reader to understand my journey for context. It can be uncomfortable to venture down a trail if you have never navigated the path before.

What motivated me? After years of working for large corporations and quasi-governmental agencies, where my talents were developed and purposefully utilized to benefit the interest of these firms turned out to be a good source of motivation. I watched how I made other people ahead of me in the organizational hierarchy successful at my expense. I am always motivated to prove myself worthy. I draw on years of coming up from the bottom and rising to the top. My problem was always having someone higher, but insecure in their own abilities, trying to knock me down for being acknowledged for my accomplishments.

I know what it is like to be hungry and neglected. Despite my large biological family, they did not prevent me from going hungry and walking around the neighborhood unsupervised. We lived on the other side of the railroad tracks so to speak. I recall my younger brothers and me making mayonnaise sandwiches or sugar sandwiches on white bread. There are things as a child I should have never seen but was forced to witness and move on as if nothing happened. When my parents were sober, we ate, our home was cleaned, and our clothes washed. Otherwise, there were many nights we were left alone or with strangers. I never felt afraid to be alone in that four-square mile of Inkster. The town was more rural then, with many roads unpaved, and people farmed in Westland, the town just across the street from our home. Even though my family was well-known, there were times when I was neglected. My walks would take me through various neighborhoods where my other family members lived. I was like a character in the Mark Twain, Adventures of Huckleberry Finn. Although in my case, I met poor black and white hobos along the Michigan Avenue railroad tracks. Perhaps it was a different time, or people in the community had sympathy for me because of my influential family. Some family members would feed me, like my sweet Aunt Bay, while others would send me on my way. I often made my way to the Texaco Service station owned by grandfather, where I rubbed oil on my hands and walked amongst the workers with a shop towel in my back pocket. I always helped myself to potatoes chips from the snack rack and candy bars from the display case. My grandfather exclaimed his displeasure to my father, only to enrage my father's rebuttal that I could have whatever the F#&@ I wanted. The confrontations between my parents were frequent and became more violent. My state of family bliss came to an end when the department of social services removed us from the care of our parents. As the social workers gathered our things, I can recall one saying to the other that five molded hotdogs were in the refrigerator.

Upon arriving at the foster home, and eventually placed in the care of Ms. White, my life would never be the same. Between social services supervised visits with my biological mother and the funeral of my biological father, I lost all hope of ever reuniting with my family. I felt abandoned and isolated. I spent so much of my life, running away from my past, resentful, angry, and ashamed of being poor. I suffered from deep depression because of the traumatic experience at such a young age. I never received psychological therapy or mental health care. I had to adjust to my new environment. Ms. White was tough on me, and while I did not appreciate her tactics in raising me, when I look back, I am grateful for her in preparing me to survive. While there was no drinking and smoking at Ms. White's house, it was just as dysfunctional; given the various people she let lived in the three-bedroom house to help her pay bills. Her home was like a boarding house at times. I had an innate mechanical mind and the ability to draw. These gifts would enable me to work and earn money to become independent from Ms. White's control.

We moved to northwest Detroit at the height of White flight to the suburbs, and many of my friends lived in homes with well-manicured yards.

During the transition, I had German, Jewish and Polish friends. I saw all the well-dressed boys who attended Detroit Catholic Central High School being picked up by their parents. I often wondered if I could be like them. But I soon learned the odds are stacked against anyone living in poverty, and highly unlikely of living the American dream. Throughout my life, I had to start out on the bottom. I was blessed because I rose from poverty to become a productive member of society. While my success did not come without some help from others along the way, it wasn't based on luck. I had to be prepared when the opportunities became available. Despite the opportunity, I still had to overcome and persevere against systemic racism and social bias, educational limitations, corporate nepotism, as well as my own personal defects.

My street education and academic curriculums provided the connections I needed to make sense of the world. During grade school, I was taught about colors, numbers, birds, and the bees. In middle school, I learned African Americans were inferior people originating from slaves and White people were intellectually superior from the beginning of time. In high school, I learned Black people lived in communities with gangs and high crime, poverty, and other struggles in their lives, while White people were building wealth, expanding safe drug-free suburb communities, and enriching their lives. When I entered college, I learned it was all lies. The African continent is made up of a diverse group of people and rich history. I was forced to endure images of Black people portrayed as heathens, servants, criminals, or men with timid minds who exhibited child-like behavior. I vowed this will not be me. I had to work twice as hard for recognition than my White counterpart. And in most cases, my work was credited to my White supervisor, and so accepting their White privilege as normal weighed on me. To feel good about myself, I tried to keep up with the Jones, buying a big home with a well-groom lawn, new cars, giving my children cellphones, and sending them to exclusive sport camps. I lost sight of what was important. Even though I was told by my elders growing up it would be like this, I still let envy and resentment consume me. I became a functioning alcoholic until I could no longer manage it. I lost nearly all the material things I worked so hard to acquire. My wife and children suffered too. While life's challenges were exacerbated by my alcoholism, my life's challenges were liberating after I got sober and recovered. If only I learned early on that I will never have control over other people, places, and things, how far along I might have been. But that' part of my life's journey. The gift of sobriety enabled me to accept me for who I am and not what others define me to be was huge. I was given a second chance to live out my purpose, and that is to be of service to humanity. I continue to work hard because I am the type of person driven by results. I am not a slave to material things but will work to get what I need. There's a saying *"religious people pray to keep from going to hell, and spiritual people thank God for getting them through hell."* Even though I reference God regularly, I am not religious by any means, but I do believe in the power of prayer and meditation. Through my recovery, I was pruned back like a rose bush allowing me to grow stronger. I have nothing to prove, nothing to gain but to fulfill my small part by sharing my story, and perhaps inspire someone else greater blessings to make it real.

It's important for the reader to understand my strengths and struggles. I learned that you cannot move forward with your life until you accept you have a problem.

When did I get inspired to speak out? I have always expressed my opinion. As a youngman, my opinions were baseless and unsubstantiated. It was like erecting a building on a sandy foundation. As I got older, I only used verified facts to support my position. Before I go about making claims about what's right or wrong with America's capitalism, one must have clean hands. When I speak about a company start up or a CEO building his or her team, it is important that they hire the best people who can help them drive the business and achieve financial results. These people are very visible, and their worth must be quantifiable, believe me, I speak from experience. Since I worked outside the C-suite bubble most of my career, I often felt empty and unfulfilled when I saw privileged people up close and personal.

It doesn't matter if you are Black or White, an American or from other countries around the world, nepotism and favoritism is unfair. It is clear why such arrangements are frowned upon in the workplace, as they present all kinds of issues. Yet, it still exists. Leaders and high-ranking managers of organizations have found ways around work-related requirements having their friends and relatives hired by and reporting to other people. Some of these people are known for working less, defying office work rules, and benefiting from inflated salaries. I worked as a leader at several corporations and witnessed leaders with high integrity to places where I have seen overtly shameless acts where unqualified friends are hired and given salaries they did not deserve or earn. I learned in my career how to delegate meaningful assignments, allocate reasonable levels of authority to employees so people can make decisions, and hold individuals accountable for delivering results. As an African American man nearing the twilight of his career, trying to debate White privilege is futile. Black entrepreneur leaders must build their own way around these circumstances, and be above reproach.

I do not want to see the development of up-and-coming Black organizations grow and prosper, only to fall short by following the same patterns. These types of organizations cannot and will not attract and maintain the best talent. They are only designed to exploit talented people until they leave. Many unsavory firms got wealthy by identifying good African American talent, paying them less than their value, extract everything out of them, and then discard them. It happened in the music industry, professional sports and it happened to me personally. Today, musicians are establishing their own record labels, sport agents work for the professional athlete, and fortune 500 corporations are actively recruiting African Americans from top universities. All things being the same, if an African American conglomerate is formed, they must be willing to recruit high quality African American candidates and compensate them accordingly. I was trusted to represent fortune 500 companies with billions of their shareholder's monies. Would a Black company do the same?

It is one thing to stand by and watch progress pass you by when you do not understand what is happening, but it is an entirely different thing to stand by when you know what is happening and being powerless to do anything about it. When President Obama made what was considered a Gaffe, when the insinuated people who claimed they built their companies, saying

"*You didn't build that*", but when put into context, he meant people didn't build their companies without the help of the government infrastructure or other people helping them along the way. Of course, it takes hard work to start, manage, and maintain a successful company, President Obama was correct! If we could examine some of these so-called self-built success stories, you will find they all probably got a little help along the way.

It is also common for there to be closed shops for certain industrial sectors throughout the world, including the U.S. In most cases, it comes down to scale, then experience and the ability to execute. We live in a society of laws that protect our way of life and having laws in place to protect our innovation and ingenuity is a good thing. The use of patents, via the U.S. Patent Office (proprietary properties) represents one legal instrument to control new entry of products in the market. The infrastructure market is highly regulated, and compliance of federal, state, and municipal codes are designed to protect society, which means only certain qualified entities, knowledgeable of rigid standards and possess the necessary technical expertise to manage and deliver goods and services on a large-scale. The more sinister and egregious barriers come from self-proclaimed local ordinances designed to impose minimum qualifications that are tailored to certain firms and disqualify other firms based on a narrow set of standards that are only attainable to a few firms. If the purpose is to dictate who can enter the market, then the game is rigged to a certain extent unless you have power to overcome barriers.

In today's political climate, being a Republican is an anathema, constantly being associated with White nationalist and racist. Conversely, the so-called "woke" Democrat Party is no different. Both parties are controlled by White majorities and set the ground rules for engagement. Regardless of which party is in control of White House, the U.S. Congress, in most cases, real influence comes down to who control the state government. As political pundits say, politics are local. If enough people come together, they can decide how to influence one political party over another. It happened to the GOP with the avid of President Trump, and continues to trickle down to the states like Michigan. During my life, I have established credibility, forming relationships between both parties. I understood how to navigate and avoid the common irritations at the core of each camp. I can tell you from personal experience, I don't care who is in charge, when Black people possess the means to influence, both parties will fall inline. A lobbyist gives certain people access to the decision-makers who make decisions and draft legislation. While we do not consider lobbyist a function of quid pro quo (pay to play), the game is rigged to a certain extent.

Once you earn the respect of the private investors, politicians, and the American people then there is an argument for reparations. In my role as a leader of an organization where I had influence, I sought ways to give underrepresented communities access to public contracts. I helped develop a narrative to engage these communities and inform them about barriers to contracts, limited by ordinances and certification requirements. To qualify for a contract with a municipality, a firm must adhere to a set of guidelines, supposedly designed to promote fairness. The process has nothing to do with getting the best value, finding the best firm, or even promoting inclusion. Most municipal ordinances were most likely drafted by attorneys, with little input from businesspeople. I found critical decisions being made by bureaucrats who mindlessly check the box, stamp the paper, and closeout the file. As long as politicians can appoint political cronies to key posts, accompanied by all kinds of private overtures, there will always be this swinging of the pendulum to accommodate preferential treatment by a particular faction. It is amazing how petty some people are, especially people appointed to power, can have a profoundly debilitating effect on people of color and their community.

It's important for the reader to understand my sense of timing. I learned that an inability to question one's own null hypothesis of truth is destined for failure, and only comes with experience and preparation.

Why did I feel compelled to write this book? I feel like my time is running out, and I need to make amends for my delay. Even though I recovered from my shortcomings, I continue to strive for perfection, and set high expectations for myself – a serious defect. I am constantly driven and focused on making progress. The higher the role I have held in an organization, the more I wanted to prove I could do the job. Regardless of whether

I worked in the private sector or the government sector, I would encounter mediocrity. Working in quasi-government agencies was the worst because there are more opportunities for the people who are "takers' to hide and receive credit for doing the least, while the people who are "givers" did most of the work and received little to no recognition. And of course, you had to deal with those dreaded politicians. My greatest defect of character is overcoming my selfishness; learning to forget and forgive those who wronged me. My wife insisted that I would never be happy working for someone else because people never measured up to my standards or someone would always seem to disappoint me. I have no interest in being popular, and my love for humanity is not limited to any race of people, culture, or religious edict. In our society, humanity always needs an enemy. In my opinion, evil thoughts are the enemy; and victory over our enemy is dispelling evil thought. It is because of my faith; I believe anything is possible! This manifesto is my contribution to family, community, and country. When I think of family, it's not about people who are necessarily blood related. I was literally raised by a village, as parents of childhood friends, teachers and people in the community shared their time and resources. They corrected me when I misbehaved and praised me when I did a good deed. Many of the opportunities afforded to me came through the kindness of White people. And to those individuals, I owe a great deal of thanks and gratitude. It was never about getting rich at all costs for me; while I may not be athletic and I cannot sing; I was more than capable dealing drugs, living the gang culture and selling religion. There were a few successful people in the drug game that were able to transfer their riches into legitimate enterprises, going from rapping to acting and marketing private label alcoholic beverages, fragrances, and clothing lines. Even though misguided, some have gone on to support worthy charitable social causes. Of course, there are those nationally recognized pastors and ministers of televised evangelical mega-churches who built their own little religious kingdoms. Some of these churches have done great work, from establishing international ministries in sub-Sahara African countries to providing domestic economic development opportunities in neighborhoods surrounding their churches. However, African American families and communities still languish in the shadows. Clearly, benevolence alone will not be enough, and that include government set asides. When I talk about reparations, it is not about getting a check from the United States Treasury. While Affirmative Action legislation, welfare and other social services started out with good intentions, they failed African Americans because they only created dependency, victims, and did nothing to restore their dignity and ability to achieve self-determination. We need to promote new social norms in Black people that rely less on conspiracy theories and focus more on facts. There are numerous examples of African Americans making attempts to provide a common social construct, from Kwanzaa, a seven-day holiday celebration to uplift African Americans founded in 1966, by Maulana Ndabezitha Karenga (born, Ronald McKinley Everett), to the Isuthu Institute, founded by Reverend Wendell Anthony, the esteemed pastor of Fellowship Chapel Church in Detroit, Michigan, who published the Handbook of the Isuthu Institute, outlining the passage from young men and woman to adulthood. African American reparations is part of the zeitgeist of the 2000's. We must instill principles that will resonate with the politics and belief systems of the American people in a meaningful way. The African American community is not limited to inner-city neighborhoods. Black people live in every quarter of the United States; hence, our physical communities are boundless. However, I think a Basecamp (e.g., nucleus) if you will is needed, from which a moral compass originates and personify the common goals of Black people to help change America for the good of the country.

People in America are hurting, especially people of color. From all accounts, America's brand will continue to decline and lose the gold standard for the land of opportunity unless the psyche of the people changes. If we continue to live in doubt and fear of one another, it can only lead to resentment and despair. We must learn to live in peace and restore hope. People are asking what life will be like after COVID-19. The answer is life will go on! Most of us were not around in 1918, during the last world pandemic. It was called the Spanish Flu, and what followed was the roaring 1920's. Today, the anxiety of America and western countries in general is rooted in divisiveness, sparked in part, by fear amongst White Nationalist. The enemy wants to divide people along racial ideological lines; with the genesis being immigration at its origin. I believe we need to move towards forgiveness and combat this so-called enemy with the determination to foster our own version of America, as it is not up to racist to define it for us. The energy required to fuel hate and revenge is counterproductive. Knowledge of our system of governance, wisdom stemming from building relationships across cultures, ethnicities and religious traditions, and persistence in creating a positive message is the winning formula. I believe human interactions and the need for serious relationship must rebound. I believe America could embark on another roaring 20's that followed Spanish Flu, only in this case is the new roaring 2020's, following the Coronavirus. We must resolve our deep-seated human conflicts and reengage interpersonal relationships to prevent people from living in ideological bubbles. The earth is not dying, but the people who inhabit the earth might die off as the human population exceeds the earth's carrying capacity to support them. According to scientists, with the rise in human population and the rate of fossil fuel consumption needed to manufacture food production, transport people and goods is not sustainable. Therefore, ignoring climate change is not an option or a solution.

There are no boundaries when it comes to human innovation. It is not exclusive to a certain type of person, people, or country. However, the person, people or country must be open to changing their mindset to receive the new idea. Human advancement from ancient times hitherto has constantly undergone transformations based on knowledge and wisdom. The early ancients believed the stars were celestial and supernatural, until later societies developed ways to record cyclical events as a predictive and measurable phenomenon. Eventually, future societies developed alphabets, language, and mathematics to translate and transfer knowledge. It took nearly 2 million years for the world population to reach 1 billion people from prehistoric times to 200 years ago. Within the last 200 years the world population is approaching 7.8 billion people, making the world a smaller place to live. Human ingenuity must explore the far reaches of our universe to seek alternative life sustaining options to support people, whether on satellite space colonies or on earth. We must find a new enemy to prevent the extinction of human beings. The survival of the human species is a result of contribution from multi-culturalism throughout the ages. We must learn to accept our differences to ensure we advance human life. When I think of future possibilities, I think about my grandson, Ra. I believe, given the opportunity, he could help change the future. It is my hope there will be a village around to help him. I pray the decade ahead will reveal God's favor upon future generations, and that is why I want to do all I can to help make it a reality. Like the children of Israel, we must adorn the children with fine clothing and jewels so that they will learn how not to live as victims.

It's important for the reader to understand I am my brother's keeper. I have an obligation to do my part to advance my family, my community, and my country – it's their choice to accept it.

A CALL TO ACTION

So, now what? This call to action is different from "The Covenant" introduced by Travis Smiley. Instead – this call to action is a brief easy-to-read less academic and common-sense approach to African American reparations. Reconciliation will never happen without the support of the American people, especially Black people. The real challenge is, is it enough to convince the most prosperous African Americans to defy the statistical improbability and join the conversation? Their participation is key to help shape a common vision for African Americans and devise a roadmap for reparations and reconciliation. I am calling on notable Black people like Robert Johnson, Aliko Dangote, Mike Adenuga, Robert Smith, David Steward, Oprah Winfrey, Strive Masiyiwa, Patrice Motsepe and Michael Jordan to participate in the conversation.

We can learn a lot from great constitutional minds like former U.S. President Barrack Obama, and other constitutional scholars to help understand reparation language and provide some thoughtful legal insight and barriers at the local, state, and federal level. Some of the greatest gifts African American's provides to the world is entertainment, sports stars, great orators, and intellectual thinkers. I am calling on famous people like Jay-Z and Beyonce, LeBron James, and their peers to offer some substantial feedback. I am calling religious theologians from the major religions to discuss the moral consciousness of Black people in America. I imagine creative minds in entertainment like Clarence Avant, and other music executives, entrepreneurs, and film producers, like Tyler Perry and other thespians to take part in the conversation. I am hopeful philosophical academic thinkers like Professor Dyson, Professor Glenn Loury, Professor Cornel West, economist, Thomas Sowell and professor John McWhorter, will add significant value to the discussion.

If you choose, your responses can remain anonymous. It is more important that the response be unfiltered and organic. If people fail to express their genuine opinion, then it is unlikely we can resolve the barriers that would prevent true reparations for African Americans and reconciliation to heal the country. The real voice needed is your voice, especially the voices of the individuals who took the time to read the white papers to form an opinion for or against the ideas laid out in the book.

A DIGITAL CONVERSATION WITH THE AMERICAN PEOPLE

Your input will drive the discussion so as not to be a one-sided conversation. Monitoring online activities and reporting back to the American people what the various book clubs think about African American Reparations, via a repository database, including chatter from other social media platforms are essential. Editorial content management will extract responses based on structured questions provided below to help the reader participate in the solution. As a follow up, a second African American Reparations, Edition 2 will be published, capturing responses from you, the reader.

HOW IT WORKS?

You can share your comments and upload your perspective at:

https://www.bryantwholt.com

Comments will be posted so others can see your opinions. Activity analytics will notify readers about the amount of buzz.

To make it easy to share your comments, content from other online social media platforms will be monitored to ensure unsolicited viewpoints are also considered. The goal is to capture a full 360-degree perspective of the global community to bring everyone into the conversation.

POTENTIAL OUTCOMES:

- Find out what the American people had to say about African American reparations? The final analyses and report will inform us as a nation whether reconciliation is possible, and healing can ensue.
- A new publication of the *African American Reparations: Edition 2*; "America's reconciliation plan for healing the cou try" will set the stage.
- I am hopeful the American people will want to see our country remain the envy of the world, where all people can live and be all they can be, and that starts at home.

GENERAL DISCUSSION QUESTIONS

The purpose of this section is to gather basic information about the reader and learn people's thoughts about the book.

OPTIONAL:

- Book Club Name
- City, State
- Gender (s)
- Ages
- Race/Ethnicity
- Country of Origin
- Political Party Affiliation
- What made you read this book?
- What feelings did the book evoke for you?
- What is the central theme discussed in the book?
- Did any of the issues raised in the book affect your life?
- What did you like most in the book?
- What did you like the least in the book?
- What did you think about the writing style of the author?
- What did you think about the author's approach?

AFRICAN AMERICAN DIVERSITY

These are suggested questions. Please feel free to insert your own questions about complex dynamics associated with labels assigned to Black people.

- Do you believe African Americans are a diverse group?
- Do you believe the book identified the biggest challenge that prevents African American unification? If not, please elaborate.
- Do you believe African Americans are good at sports and entertainment?
- Do you trust Black people as leaders?
- Given the diversity of African Americans, is a Wakanda-style foundation possible?
- Recognizing African Americans is a microcosm of the American population, it is possible for a strong centric population?
- What will it take to galvanize wealthy, middle income and poor Blacks around a common vision for reparations?
- Do you believe in the science of evolution?
- Do you believe in divine creation?
- Do you believe in elections and democracy?
- Do you believe African Americans are all inclusive of different people?

ROLE OF WEALTHY AFRICAN AMERICANS

These are suggested questions. Please feel free to insert your own questions about the role of wealthy African Americans.

- What do you think about the idea of a Wakanda-style founder's roundtable to (organize the various Black groups) govern African American affairs?
- What do you think about the formation of an African American conglomerate?
- Are wealthy African Americans the best shepherds to steer Black people?
- How likely is it that wealthy African Americans would be willing to work together towards reparations?
- Do you believe an African American conglomerate could provide economic relief to Black communities?
- Do you believe a Wakanda-style foundation can help resolve social differences amongst African Americans?
- Do you trust Black people to administer African American reparations as outlined in the book, or would you prefer White people to administer it?
- Do you believe having an African American conglomerate succession plan would ensure assets are appropriately managed and reinvested back into Black communities?
- Do you believe consolidating the largest minority depository institutions into a national Black bank system would make them stronger?

AFRICAN AMERICAN REPARATIONS

These are suggested questions. Please feel free to insert your own questions about African American reparations; for or against.

- Do you believe the American people are ready to embrace African American reparations?
- Do you think using the U.S. Bipartisan Infrastructure Bill (BIL) to facilitate the monetary instrument for reparations is a good idea?
- Do you believe there should be some accountability to the American people to track funds, monitor projects and grade inclusion performance?
- Should the American people support African American reparations? Support your yes or no answer.
- Do you believe the passage of the African American Reparations Act of 2030 would absolve the country of its slavery past once and for all?
- Describe what African American reparations means to you?
- Describe in your own words, what reconciliation means to you?
- If passage of reparations is successful, Do African American have an obligation to help raise the standard of living for poor Whites and other poor people of color?
- The language for African American reparations will most likely be prepared by constitutional lawyers and congressional legislatures, should the American people be allowed to vote by provision?

Provision I: Define purpose, scope, and institutions

Provision II: Determine federal codes and regulatory accommodations

Provision III: Determine legal requirements for federal, state, and municipalities

AFRICAN AMERICAN POLITICS, EDUCATION, RELIGION AND MEDIA

These are suggested questions. Please feel free to insert your own questions about issues facing African American, like politics, education, religion, or their images portrayed in the media.

- If the African American Reparations Act of 2030 passed, how should Black banks invest in future educational programs?
- How likely is it for Black churches across the country to partner with an African American Interdenominational Faith Council to help support their facilities and congregants?
- Is a private African American education system based on (Isuthu/Intojane) principles a good idea?
- We are who we are, because of where we come from, and when? What must the African Americans founder's roundtable do to garner support from disenfranchised Black and White people? Answer according to each generational group listed, as they require different responses:

- The Great Generation (Born: 1901 – 1927) Age in 2020: ninety-three and older; one percent of population
- The Silent Generation (Born: 1928 – 1945) Age in 2020: seventy-five to ninety-two; eleven percent of population
- Baby Boomer Generation (Born: 1946 – 1964) Age in 2020: fifty-six to seventy-four; twenty-nine percent of population
- Generation X (Born: 1965 – 1980) Age in 2020: forty to fifty-five; twenty-six percent of population
- Millennial Generation (Born: 1981 – 1996) Age in 2020: twenty-four to thirty-nine; twenty-eight of population
- Generation Z (Born: post-millennial) Age in 2020: twenty to twenty-three; five percent of population (Largest emerging voting blocs)

- Is there a disconnect between African American elite organizations (e.g., sororities, fraternities, and debutantes) and regular Black folks?
- How much influence should the foundation have on cultural behavior?

www.ingramcontent.com/pod-product-compliance
Lightning Source LLC
LaVergne TN
LVHW022035200926
848481LV00003B/698
* 9 7 9 8 8 8 8 1 2 2 4 6 4 *